Markets, Entrepreneurs and Liberty

Markets, Entrepreneurs and Liberty:

An Austrian View of Capitalism

W. Duncan Reekie
E. P. Bradlow Professor of Business Economics
University of the Witwatersrand

ST. MARTIN'S PRESS   New York

ISBN 0-312-51533-2
Library of Congress Catalog Card Number 84-40372

Contents

Contents

Preface

When I started writing this book (at the University of Edinburgh) I was unaware of a paper which was to appear in the December 1982 issue of *Zeitschrift für die gesamte Staatswissenschaft*. That paper, written by a colleague in my new place of employment, the University of the Witwatersrand encorporates and focusses on the motivation behind the following paper. Entitled 'The Salvage of Ideas: Problems of the Revival of Austrian Economic Thought' it covers much of the ground I discuss below.

The author Professor Ludwig Lachmann, shares my motivation but, as an Austrian, has both a far superior entitlement and intellectual grounding to write in this area than I. My own dissatisfaction with the conventional paradigms of much of modern economics sprang from my training in the structure: conduct: performance (S:C:P) model of industrial organisation. Nagging doubts about the validity of that model were present in my undergraduate days when I read chapters on the 'monopoly problem' in Schumpeter's *Capitalism, Socialism and Democracy*. Schumpeter was regarded as something of a maverick in those days in the very early 1960s and the pressure to conform to undergraduate 'model answers' to ensure examination success proved stronger than my feelings of scepticism.

The seeds of doubt, however, had been sown. A few years working in industry did nothing to prevent their germination and by the time I wrote my doctoral dissertation on the economics of innovation a general 'renaissance of Schumpeter' was already underway. This re-awakened interest in Schumpeter, however, was linked very closely to the profession's desire to find a starting point to study the phenomenon of industrial Research and Development. (A topical and newsworthy area because of the 'space race' and hence a field where demand existed in terms of research funding and journal space. As a profession we willingly provided a supply of academic economic activity.) This was interesting to us and not uncomfortable; as

Schumpeter's entrepreneurs, the 'New Men' of *Business Cycles* had become 'routinised' into the R & D laboratories of extant firms it was generally felt that the S:C:P paradigm could be adapted to embrace this. By the 1970s, however, two factors had emerged which convinced me this was not so.

First, empirical studies by Brozen and Demsetz began to cast doubt on the basic S:C:P paradigm itself. Simultaneously Mansfield's work suggested that no simple one-off adaptation of that model could embrace technological change in a manner which would operate in regular, predictable fashion for any heterogeneous collection of industries or firms in real life.

Second, in 1972, Kirzner's book *Competition and Entrepreneurship* appeared. Reading it, I realised that an entire approach to economics had been denied me as a student and was still being denied most students in the English-speaking world.

My short work *Industry, Prices and Markets* (1979) was the consequence of that realisation. It related mainly to the theory of the firm and industry. It discussed the contribution which the neglected area of Austrian economics highlighted by Kirzner and the new findings of Brozen and Demsetz could make to that field.

I discovered in the process of researching that book (along with many other economists of the middle 1970s) that as a profession we had turned our backs on the methodology, the discoveries, and the theories of a whole school of economic thought, and had not done so simply in the one field of industrial organisation, as I had originally believed.

This method of approaching the discipline began, as the name implies, in Austria in the Vienna of the 1870s. It remained strongly based there until Hitler's *Anschluss*, when as Lachmann puts it, 'Vienna ceased to be an important centre of economic studies'.

The individuals concerned subsequently scattered throughout the world. (One of the most prominent, Professor Hayek, enjoyed a brief few years of fame at the London School of Economics.) The combination of their physical dispersal plus the advent, political attractiveness and, at the time, apparent intellectual success of Lord Keynes' 'New Economics' over some of Hayek's views resulted in the eclipse of Austrianism. Hayek devoted himself to work on political philosophy at the University of Chicago and from 1949, Lachmann laments, 'the next 25 years or so were . . . Wilderness' years.

Professor Kirzner in New York University worked with Professor

Mises, an immigrant from Vienna. But Mises was becoming increasingly elderly. As Professor Kirzner himself confided to me, the decade of the 1960s was an extremely 'lonely' one for him.

Yet by the late 1970s 'Austrianism' was again a word in the vocabulary of economists of all shades of opinion and fields of study. It was no longer an arcane area examined only by specialists in the development of economic thought. Professor Hayek received the Nobel Prize in Economics in 1974. He has now returned to writing and lecturing in economics as such. Professor Kirzner is universally regarded as the leader of a worldwide group of scholars and 'loneliness' is no longer a word which is of relevance to him.

This book is an attempt to explain some of the reasons for this remarkable transformation. Unlike my earlier *Industry, Prices and Markets* it is not confined to only one area of study. Because the Austrians have themselves linked economics with political philosophy (in the best tradition of Adam Smith) this linkage is reflected in the following pages. An attempt is made to lead the reader from the beginnings of Austrianism in the 1870s, to its decline in the period 1930–70. This is done in Chapters 1 and 2. Chapter 2 will be familiar to readers trained before the mid-1970s as a simplified version of the economic othodoxy we grew up with.

Chapters 3 and 4 basically describe the Austrian approach which (historically) was swamped by the orthodoxy described in Chapter 2. But these chapters and Chapter 5 indicate how and why Austrianism has again become a research programme for economists, now that the neo-classical orthodoxy of Chapter 2 is no longer universally accepted. Finally in the last three chapters some of the more recent Austrian and neo-Austrian developments in economics, in the theory of trade and exchange, of bureaux and politics, and on moral philosophy are examined.

Austrianism can no longer be ignored. The development of my own thought over the years convinces me of this. The last four chapters of the book suggest by inference that it may become one important trend of liberal, market economic thought. I believe that in the future it will be synthesised with mainstream economics and not rejected by it as happened in mid-century. It will no longer exist in isolation. In the process, however, by so leavening mainstream economics, and in being so radically different from certain areas of the mainstream, economics itself may be split into two philosophically divergent disciplines: the more-or-less liberal and the more-or-less *dirigiste*. This is a personal view I do not develop below but I suspect most readers, if they persevere to the end of the essay will come to some sort of not dissimilar conclusion.

I offer this book to undergraduate students as a means of easy access to these fascinating debates of the last decade. They will see that Austrianism does not simply represent one side of the 'Keynesianism: monetarism' issue they have seen discussed in textbooks such as Samuelson and Lipsey. I also offer this book to fellow academics, not as an original contribution, but as a quick way to find out 'what all the fuss has been about'. In a world of ever-increasing specialisation few of us have time to read the original articles in every field of our very wide profession. This is intended as a low cost route through the now voluminous Austrian and neo-Austrian literature. My aim is to whet the appetites of some readers to pursue the concepts mentioned here in depth. I will then consider my own progress from initial admiration of the neo-classical synthesis, to disenchantment, to admiration of the price mechanism (which to paraphrase Keynes 'only one man in a million understands') as having been worthwhile.

My thanks are due to Professors Mark Casson and Stephen Littlechild for having read parts of the draft. No blame for error or poverty of exposition attaches to them.

W Duncan Reekie
Johannesburg 1984

Acknowledgements

Figures 4.1–4.7 are reprinted from Garrison: 'Austrian Macro-economics: A Diagrammatical Explanation' in *New Directions in Austrian Economics*, ed. L M Spadaro. Copyright, 1978, The Institute for Humane Studies. Reprinted with permission of Andrews, McMeel & Parker. All rights reserved.

Figure 5.4 is reprinted from S C Littlechild: 'Misleading Calculation of the Social Costs of Monopoly Power', *Economic Journal*, 1981, by kind permission of Cambridge University Press.

Table 6.1 is reprinted from O E Williamson: 'Transaction Cost Economics: The Governance of Contractual Relations', *Journal of Law & Economics*, © 1979, University of Chicago Press. All rights reserved.

1 The Genealogy of Austrian Economics

THE DISTINCTIVENESS OF AUSTRIANISM

The Austrian School can be seen as dividing historically into four main groupings of individuals. Alternatively its distinctiveness as a school of thought can be seen as due to the stress laid on certain methodological approaches and assumptions not accepted or less heavily emphasised by other economists. In this chapter we concentrate predominantly on the former approach.

The term 'Austrians' was first used to describe the School's founder, Carl Menger (1840–1921) and those who were attracted to his teachings (formally published in his *Principles of Economics*, 1871). His main followers were Wieser (1851–1926) and Böhm-Bawerk (1851–1914). The term was coined by the German, Schmoller, a leading exponent of the then-dominant historical and inductive method in economics.

Menger and his colleagues in Vienna argued strongly for the deductive rather than the inductive approach to economic analysis. In deduction a set of axioms or self-evident truths is accepted and logic and *a priori* reasoning are then applied to consider the impact of a change in extraneous conditions upon them. Clearly, for practical application the premises must be realistic and the logical reasoning accurate. When the inductive method is applied attempts are made to infer general principles or laws from observations of reality. With this (historical) method care must be taken to avoid the *post hoc ergo propter hoc* fallacy ('after this therefore because of this'), and also the ever present danger that causes beyond the observer's attention may have been responsible for the change recorded. Thus an assembly of facts either over time or across situations may be positively misleading unless one *first of all* has a theory of cause and effect, established by deduction, to contrast them with.

Littlechild (1978, pp14–5) reporting on this methodological clash suggests the battle was won by the Austrians and their views became

1

accepted simply as the conventional wisdom of the day. He cites Mises as follows:

. . . after some years all the essential ideas of the Austrian School were by and large accepted as an integral part of economic theory. About . . . [1921] . . . 'Austrian School' became the name given to an important chapter of the history of economic thought; it was no longer the name of a specific sect with doctrines different from those held by other economists.

Certainly much of what had been developed by the Austrians (other than methodology) had also been accepted elsewhere. Menger, and later Böhm-Bawerk—in *Capital and Interest*, published in three volumes from 1884–1912—departed from the classical tradition of the labour theory of value. The Austrians replaced this with subjective marginal utility theory. But widespread acceptance of this 'Austrian' development is not too surprising since simultaneously (and independently) Menger in Vienna, Jevons in the UK in his *Theory of Political Economy* (1871) and the Frenchman Walras in his *Elements of Political Economy* (1874–7) were all using individual and subjective valuations as the starting point for the derivation of relative market prices.

In like manner, Böhm-Bawerk's work showing that subjective valuations will be different when there is a time factor present preceded Fisher's *Rates of Interest* (1907) by only a brief period. Böhm-Bawerk argued that differences in valuation between immediately consumable goods and goods consumable in the future is the only ultimate explanation of 'unearned' income, i.e. of interest.

The question is obviously begged: Does Austrianism persist? If so, what is distinctive about the Austrian approach and why is it so? The answer to the first question is affirmative and the justification can again be provided by reference to both personalities and the history of ideas.

The second group of Austrians were taught by the first, again domiciled originally in Vienna. They included Mises (1881–1973), and Hayek (born 1899). For at least the first half of the twentieth century they and their colleagues carried on, developed and refined the basic Austrian traditions but, unlike their predecessors, they were largely ignored by fellow economists. Mises published his *Theory of Money and Credit* in 1912. In it he built on Menger's strongly held view that money was not the product of any legislative act nor did it depend on such an act. The value of money according to the 'regression theorem' (Mises 1971 pp110–24) depends on usefulness and scarcity; the underlying factors of subjective marginal utility for any good. The demand for money today (even if only paper notes) is dependent on yesterday's purchasing power of that money. Yesterday's purchasing power depended on yesterday's money demand which in turn was affected by yet earlier purchasing power. Thus at the very inception of monetary demand the purchasing power of a certain quantity of, say, gold or silver was exclusively determined by its non-monetary uses, i.e. by its industrial valuation or demand. In short, money is not different from other commodities. Its demand, like the demand for any good, is not unlimited but is reflected by individual willingness to forego other goods and services to obtain it. Menger and Mises, having established money's similarity to goods in general thus argued against its monopolisation by government as a special case. Mises in particular argued that the consequence of such a monopolisation is an inevitable departure from 'sound money' followed by inflation and subsequent slump. Lord Robbins wrote in the Introduction to the English edition of Mises' book, that the author had had the 'melancholy satisfaction' of seeing his predictions of the post-World War I inflations and sequential Great Depression 'abundantly verified'.

In his own Preface to the 1952 edition Mises wrote 'great inflations are . . . government made . . . the boom they create is short-lived and must inevitably end in a slump . . . the demagogue may even boast of his neglect of the long-run effects. In the long-run, he repeats, we are all dead . . . but . . . we have outlived the short-run and have now come to face the long-run consequences.'

There were two main and inter-related reasons why the Austrians were neglected in the period stretching from approximately 1920 to 1970. First, the main economic problem of the 1920s and 1930s was, as Mises had forecast, inflation and then unemployment. The great John Maynard (later Lord) Keynes wrote two important books in this period. *The Treatise on Money* in 1930 was prefaced by Keynes with the remark that no single work was available which comprehensively covered the topic. Either Keynes was unaware of Mises, or as Keynes himself admitted with regret, he rarely read in German since his knowledge of that language was adequate only to comprehend ideas he already understood and was not strong enough to assimilate novel thoughts. In *The General Theory* (1936) Keynes had obviously come across the recently translated book by Mises, but he awarded it only a one page mention, almost as an afterthought, in the Appendix to Chapter 14.

The ignorance of English-speaking economists about the Austrians during this period was reinforced by the intellectual victory of Keynes' views. Although writers such as Frank Knight in the USA and Sir Dennis Robertson and Hayek (by this time at the London School of Economics) in the UK challenged Keynes from several stances his theories emerged triumphant. The political attractiveness of Keynesianism ensured that it dominated textbooks and policy making for around a quarter of a century after World War II.

The second and connected reason for the eclipse of the Austrians during this period was that Keynesian economics was essentially directed at the problems of managing economic aggregates. The problems of varying individual information, uncertainty and lack of knowledge towards which Hayek was devoting much of his effort in his study of the price system in the subjectivist and individualistic Austrian tradition, were not deemed either critical for society nor useful for the career advancement of economists. Moreover, while statistical aggregates lend themselves to mathematical manipulation the study of individual human action is not so amenable to this approach. Given the increasing use of mathematics and econometrics by economists in the 1950s and 1960s the generally non-mathematical Austrian approach tended to be ignored.

The revival of Austrianism can be dated to the early 1970s. Disillusion with Keynesianism was setting in and was epitomised by the debate between 'Keynesians' and 'monetarists' (led by Professor Friedman). Not that Austrians are or ever were monetarists in the Friedman sense: a slowly and consistently growing money supply managed by government is not at all what Menger, Mises or Hayek would argue for. The title of Hayek's 1976 book *Denationalisation of Money* is sufficiently self-explanatory to justify this statement at this juncture.

In 1974 Hayek was awarded the Nobel Prize in economics and he is the obvious elder statesman of the modern Austrian School. This third group of Austrians has its physical and intellectual headquarters in New York University. Its leader, Israel Kirzner, along with Murray Rothbard, was one of many students who attended the famous weekly seminars given by Mises in New York throughout the 1950s and 1960s. (Mises, Hayek, Machlup, Morgenstern, Schumpeter and Haberler are only some of the economists of Austrian origin who

4

emigrated to the UK or, predominantly, the USA in the face of the National Socialist takeover of Austria and Germany in the 1930s.) Now, apart from the New York group others throughout America and Europe are 'rediscovering' Austrianism or salient aspects of it.

The reader will now have noted three main groups of individuals: Menger and his colleagues, Mises and Hayek, and currently Hayek, Kirzner and their associates. This chapter opened with a reference to four distinct historical strands in Austrianism. The fourth was neglected until Rothbard (1976, pp52–6) pointed out the Aristotelian and Scholastic roots of the Austrians. In the fifth book of the *Nicomachean Ethics*, Aristotle argues that justice in trade requires an 'exchange of equivalents'. Thomas Aquinas in a commentary on this suggested that equivalence should be interpreted in terms of costs, and mainly labour costs at that. And yet Aquinas also, paradoxically, insisted that all goods are valued only in relation to human wants. From this the Scholastics developed the term 'just price' as a moral conception of the value of a good to the community. Rothbard (1976, p55) quotes Saravìa (a Spanish Scholastic of the mid-1500s) as stating that the 'just price is found not by counting the cost but by common estimation'. And Blaug (1968, p37) reminds us that 'Aristotle himself stands at the head of both traditions in value theory, namely utility theory and the theory of labour value. Thus while the Scholastics and Aristotelians never fully accepted the labour theory of value they came close to accepting and discovering marginal utility theory. The classical economists from Smith and Ricardo through to Marx and his followers travelled the labour cost route suggested by the ambiguous treatment of value by Aristotle and the Scholastics. The achievement of the early Austrians was to remove this ambiguity by resolving the 'paradox of value'. They did not discover utility theory as such, this had already been done; rather they developed and refined it *via* the route of marginalism.

PLAN AND PURPOSE

We have now examined, albeit somewhat superficially, the Austrian methodology, and the genealogy, by personalities, of Austrian economics. The Appendix gives further brief biographical notes on some of the individuals referred to above.

Chapter 2 details the development of orthodox economics, both micro and macro from Marshall, through Keynes and Chamberlin to Phillips. No pretence is made that this is a definitive account of the development of economic thought over that 60 year period. However, providing what is a brief overview of the economic orthodoxy taught to students during the 1950s and 1960s enables us to illustrate how economics departed from, indeed became inconsistent with, the Austrian advances of Menger and his later followers.

In Chapters 3 and 4 the alternative Austrian developments, at a micro and macro level respectively, are exposited. The Austrian insights on method, on the equilibrating role of prices (as opposed to price equilibrium), and on the place of money in the economy are all linked with individual names such as Mises and Hayek, Menger and Böhm-Bawerk. Just as the individuals were neglected so were the ideas. Chapters 3 and 4 resurrect some of these ideas, not as a novelty, but rather replicating (or less modestly, assisting) in the process of what Lachmann describes as their 'salvage'. Chapter 4 concludes by examining how, for expository purposes, modern Austrians such as Garrison have managed to reconcile some elements of Keynesianism with Hayekian macro-economics.

Chapter 5 builds on the microeconomics of Chapter 3 (with which Austrians are most at home) and examines the notions of Kirzner and Hayek on competition as a process. The recent near reconciliation of Kirzner's views on entrepreneurship with those of Schumpeter are detailed. In Chapter 6 the very thorny problem of identifying the entrepreneur is tackled. Is he the capitalist? Is he any one of us? Can he be conceptually isolated? Kirzner has provided answers to which we weld the modern neo-Austrian theories of transaction costs of Coase and Williamson. We discover that a single answer is impossible. We are all entrepreneurs, yet the market in corporate control makes some of us relatively active and some of us relatively passive players of the entrepreneurial role. Here there is still work to be done to clarify thought and avoid confusion.

Chapter 7 highlights one area where that confusion of role, by the role players themselves, is most likely. This is the area of state controlled bureaucracy. In one sense the presence of bureaux is helpful to the analyst since it adds clarity to the nature of what an entrepreneur is outside the bureaucratic setting. But does it help us more with concepts than with applications?

Chapter 8 follows on in a normative but logical fashion suggesting that bureaucracy stifles entrepreneurship. A society based on private property rights is, it is argued, not the best, but simply the best of all possible worlds where other possible worlds, such as state bureaucracy, are worse. A haunting question is begged: do property rights, by which Austrian theory is underpinned, involve duties or obligations? The Austrian who wishes to follow the logic, in uncompromising Misesian fashion, is forced to admit that property rights assume personal greed, but that personal greed results in more frequent and greater numbers of mutually satisfactory exchanges between individuals than does bureaucracy, which either stifles greed motivated exchange by individuals, or encourages (and legislates for) greed motivated non-voluntary exchange situations by organised groups in society at the expense of the non-organised individuals who comprise that society. These conclusions will not be welcomed by all readers of this book. But it is to these conclusions that we find ourselves pushed by the logic of our own arguments. If we are to be dissuaded from believing the conclusions to be valid we must also ask, in fairness, that our detractors show us where our logic is in error.

REFERENCES

M Blaug, *Economic Theory in Retrospect*, Heinemann, 1968.
S C Littlechild, *The Fallacy of the Mixed Economy*, Hobart Paper No 80, Institute of Economic Affairs, 1978.
L von Mises, *The Theory of Money and Credit*, Foundation for Economic Education, 1971.
M Rothbard, 'New Light on the Prehistory of the Austrian School' in E G Dolan (ed), *The Foundations of Modern Austrian Economics*, Sheed and Ward, 1976.

2 The Rise of Marshallian Neo-Classicism and Keynesian Orthodoxy

The rejection of classical economics by the neo-classical marginalists after 1870 did not proceed in a uniform manner throughout the world. Despite Mises' assertion that Austrianism had become the received view (p 2 above) Kirzner (1981, pp 113–6) argues that there was 'little international cross-fertilization' before World War I. Intellectually, Marshall succeeded Jevons in Britain. Pareto in Lausanne developed the work of Walras, and in the USA J B Clark pursued his own line. Despite the common starting points in each of these cases (the role of the consumer, of marginal utility and of the demand side of markets) Kirzner points out that only the Austrians failed to be diverted away from further and direct development of these initiatives of the 1870s.

AUSTRIANS AND THE OTHER MARGINALIST SCHOOLS

For both the Marshallians and the Walrasians economics came more and more to be a study of markets in equilibrium. Arrival at equilibrium itself was regarded at best as the achievement of some hypothetical decision maker and at worst (from the Austrian viewpoint) as a condition already attained: a given. Walras used the concept of *tatonnement* where an imaginary auctioneer continuously adjusted prices until the market clearing price was reached. Marshall, contrariwise, focussed on quantity adjustments to arrive at equilibrium in his supply and demand diagrams. Ultimately economics everywhere was to concentrate more and more not just on one market, but generally over all markets. Austrians balked at this on at least three grounds.

First, although study of general equilibrium theory proved to be intellectually stimulating for its own sake it also proved extremely amenable to mathematical analysis. Wieser (of the original Austrians) had already objected to the use of mathematical methodology in the subject on the grounds that economic phenomena are necessarily discontinuous and discrete and consequently not tractable by the calculus. Second, study of general equilibrium inevitably and explicitly involved the use of statistical aggregations of subjective concepts of value. The summation of logically dissimilar elements was unacceptable to the Austrians. Third, competition came to take on a meaning wholly different to what it had implied to earlier writers such as Adam Smith, and indeed to all laymen, and was used to define the *state* of equilibrium, 'perfect competition', rather than the *process* of reaching that equilibrium. As a consequence the entrepreneur as a key figure in that process was ignored by all but the Austrians. Likewise the commodity of information, which Austrians regard as a costly good which can assist the competitive process and which becomes freely available as a *consequence* of that process was seen by mainstream economists not as a consequence but as a *condition* of 'perfectly competitive equilibrium'.

MARGINALISTS AND CLASSICISTS

The classical economists from Smith to Mill were predominantly interested in the 'Wealth of Nations', where wealth was measured by goods, and not, as in Mercantilist days, by the accumulation of precious metals in the hands of a strong, centralised State. The source of wealth lay in labour, specialisation and freedom of trade and exchange. In the very first words of his Introduction Smith (1976, p104) argues for labour value theory:

The annual labour of every nation is the fund which originally supplies it with all . . . it annually consumes, and which consists always either in the immediate produce of that labour, or in what is purchased with that produce from other nations.

This is followed by Smith's famous discussion of the advantages of the division of labour and free and self-interested trade and exchange (pp117–9).

This division of labour, from which so many advantages are derived, is not originally the effect of any human wisdom, which foresees and intends that general opulence to which it gives occasion. It is the necessary, though very

9

slow and gradual consequence of a certain propensity in human nature which has in view no such extensive utility; *the propensity to truck, barter and exchange* one thing for another . . . this propensity . . . *belongs not to our present subject to inquire* . . . [but it] is not from the benevolence of the butcher, the brewer, or the baker that we expect our dinner, but from their regard to their own interest. We address ourselves, not to their humanity but to their self-love, and never talk to them of our necessities but of their advantages (emphases added).

Both Austrians and mainstream neo-classical economists would find much to agree with but also much to disagree with in these Smithian doctrines. Both would baulk at his acceptance of the labour theory of value. They would accept that division of labour leads to exchange. The Austrians would argue, against Smith, that 'the propensity to truck, barter and exchange' is definitely a prime subject of study: namely who is and what is an entrepreneur? Why, when and how does he facilitate or initiate exchange? The neo-classicists would agree with the Austrians that exchange should not be ignored. They would adopt the view that the marginalist revolution, just as it had removed the labour theory of value as an explanation for utility, had also provided the rationale for the occurrence of truck and trade. Unlike the Austrians, however, they would not see the study of the entrepreneur as of importance. Rather they would view the entrepreneur as some sort of *deus ex machina* which had brought about a historical exchange: the current result of which is of more importance for study than the means which had brought it about.

Before examining the Austrian developments further, however, the mainstream evolution of thought from the classical starting point will be surveyed.

The non-Austrian part of the marginalist revolution provided the already extant classical insights with a rationale for the process of exchange. It provided rules as to why and when exchange would take place. It enabled Pareto to develop the concept of 'economic man' and Lionel (later Lord) Robbins (1935, p16) could write that economics is then 'the science which studies human behaviour as a relationship between ends and means which have alternative uses'. This problem then merely requires that ends and means be known or given (a state of affairs which Austrians would deem impossible) following which a mathematical calculation can be performed to find the allocation of resources which must exist so that the marginal rates of substitution between any two commodities or factors be the same in all their different uses.

But this is to advance too far too fast. What the marginalists initially achieved was to resolve the paradox of value, dethrone the labour theory of value and make relative prices and relative scarcities the foundations of neo-classical economics. The development of a framework of equilibrium rules for the optimal allocation of available resources then became the chief end of non-Austrian economic thinkers.

THE EQUILIBRIUM OF THE NON-AUSTRIAN MARGINALISTS

The behavioural assumption underlying neo-classical economics is that man is a utility maximiser. Moreover, this utility can be 'approximately measured by [a] sum of money'. (Marshall, 1966, p13). Certainly Marshall admitted that money is valued more highly by some than by others 'but these differences may generally be neglected when we consider the average of large numbers of people' (pp5–6). Interestingly Marshall was still not wholly convinced that aggregation was as easy as he made out. He argued that if a £1 tax was levied on all of the citizens of Sheffield and of Leeds 'the loss of pleasure . . . is of about equal importance' in each city. But this 'probability becomes greater still if all of them are adult males engaged in the same trade; and therefore presumably similar in sensibility and temperament, in taste and education' (p16).

Marshall's helpful, but basically disregarded caveat about aggregation is, unfortunately, only enhanced by the lack of homogeneity in his choice of illustrative cities. Leeds was a leading woollen and garment centre while Sheffield, only a few miles away, was the principal locus for the steel, engineering and cutlery industries. These 'seem to be located in Sheffield for one reason only: they are all highly skilled manufactures in which the things that Sheffield men can do to the raw material make it worth while carrying that material half across England to do it' (*The Economist*, 16 January 1954).

Nevertheless Marshall remained sufficiently content with aggregation as an adequate approximation that he went on, as Bell (1981, p50) says, to develop the 'first neo-classical summation' of exchange. Using the now familiar demand and supply curves, derived from

11

marginal utility and production costs respectively, he showed how partial equilibrium and so the market clearing price were attained. Or rather he presumed to show this.

If the demand price is greater than the supply price for amounts just less than the equilibrium amount, it is sure to be less than the supply price for amounts just greater: and therefore, if the scale of production is somewhat increased beyond the equilibrium position, it will tend to return and *vice versa* (Marshall, p288).

Marshall uses his famous supply and demand cross to illustrate this in a footnote on the same page. Vertical lines are drawn to the quantity axis on either side of the equilibrium point, but no further explanation is given. The tendency towards equilibrium is explained only by the metaphorical example of a stone attached to a piece of string which gravity tends to push or pull towards equilibrium, but the erratically running waters of a mill stream in which the string is hanging result in unpredictable oscillations about the equilibrium point.

Intuitively this is less valid as an analogy than *tatonnement*, although it is in fact a little more realistic. Marshall then proceeded, and for a few sentences appeared to be on the verge of anticipating Hayek: 'But we cannot foresee the future perfectly. The unexpected may happen; and the existing tendencies may be modified before they have had time to accomplish . . . their full work . . . [since] general conditions of life are not stationary . . .' (p289).

This comment did not distract him from what he saw as his main task, however. This, the formulation of a system of general equilibrium, when the market clearing price could be established in all markets simultaneously, was tackled in Book V. Chapters v and xii. Marshall did not wholly succeed in this and the system was not perfected until Pareto derived his now famous concept of optimality.

Prior to Pareto, however, J B Clark in his *Distribution of Wealth* (1899) extended marginalism into the analysis of production and distribution and introduced the concept of the marginal product. A producer would not seek to offer an additional worker a greater wage than the value his marginal product could be sold for. Thus the numbers of workers hired would be that amount where the cost of the marginal worker equalled the value of his output, no more and no less. This principle could be extended, argued Clark, to the other factors of production such as land and capital. Under perfect competition each factor would receive a return exactly equal to its contribution, the value of the marginal product.

The whole neo-classical edifice coincided with and could be rationalised by Say's Law of Markets. J B Say, a French writer from the early nineteenth century had argued that the sum of all planned market excess demands always equals zero. Crudely put this has often been restated as 'supply creates its own demand'. Temporary gluts or shortfalls could thus occur in any market. But these would be short-lived as wages and prices adjusted in the relevant markets bringing the whole system back to general equilibrium.

But was Say's Law correct? Could a unique general equilibrium for all conceivable markets exist simultaneously? And if not were there automatic forces described analogously as a stone on a string held in running water (Marshall) or an auctioneer (Walras)?

Walras in his *Elements* (1874–77) gave a positive answer to the first question. All prices in all markets are determined simultaneously and by solving the relevant simultaneous equations the general equilibrium position can be determined. Pareto, who succeeded Walras, introduced still greater mathematical precision and abandoned the Benthamite goal of the 'greatest good of the greatest number' in favour of a solution welfare economists now call Pareto optimality. That is, a general equilibrium position where no movement is possible which can make any one person better off without making some other worse off.

The state of economic theory was thus becoming highly refined, if not rarefied and in America in particular its usefulness was being queried (Bell, 1981, p58). Four explicit non-Austrian attempts were made to connect this theory with reality. Bell (1981, pp59–69) provides a retrospective view of this period and the next four sections draw in part on his exposition. (The four attempts were the Quantity Theory of Money; the Keynesian Revolution; the Phillips Curve; and monopolistic competition. All of which, in some form, are part of any foundation course in economics.)

THE QUANTITY THEORY OF MONEY

Money was not important in the analyses of either Marshall or Walras. Blaug (1968 p427) goes so far as to accuse Marshall of a 'total neglect of monetary forces . . . [which] however much he warned his readers of this failing, did much to persuade economists that monetary theory belonged to the periphery of the science.'

Why did money occupy such an unimportant place in this period of the history of economic thought? The answer can possibly be found by examining the Walrasian *tatonnement* process more closely. In *tatonnement* money has no unique attributes. And, unlike Say's Law (which refers only to planned demands) in *tatonnement* no distinction is made between *effective* and *planned* demands. Plans are not executed and do not become effective until the auctioneer calls out all the relevant prices for general equilibrium to be accomplished. So it became normal for mathematical economists to ignore the difference between planned and effective demands in their constructions of the relevant simultaneous equation model of the economy. Under this scenario (sometimes known as Walras' Law) the sum of the money values of market excess demands (both planned and effective) is zero.

In the *tatonnement* process an excess supply of any good (not just money) is effective in putting upward pressure on the price of the good for which there is a corresponding excess demand. The auctioneer simply lowers the price he calls out for the good in excess supply and raises it for the good in excess demand. But in reality there is no auctioneer. Upward pressure on price comes about only if *money* expenditures on the good exceed the money value of planned sales. Downward pressure on prices similarly only exists (absent the auctioneer) if money expenditures are less than the money value of planned sales. Since in reality barter is rarely used money has a unique and important role to play.

It was this essential discovery, that Walras' Law referred to both planned and effective demands, which enabled Keynes to highlight the importance of 'effective demand failure' and so also of money in explaining the 1930s Depression. This point may be more readily assimilated if Say's Law is explained in more detail. The following paragraphs draw on Baird's (1977, pp49–62) exposition.

Suppose all transactors are neither thieves nor philanthropists, that is all trades are voluntary on both sides. Then anyone who plans to acquire more of something must also plan to give up something in exchange. Moreover, the market values of the two commodities must be identical (since he is neither thief nor philanthropist). His source of funds for purchasing is the market price of what he plans to give up multiplied by its quantity (for example, one hour of labour times the hourly wage rate). A source of funds is obviously essential unless the economy is in a barter state.

For any individual then, his planned uses of funds must exactly offset his planned sources of funds. So for any one individual the following equation of intentions holds:

$$p_1 \Delta q_1 + p_2 \Delta q_2 + p_3 \Delta q_3 + \ldots + p_i \Delta q_i + \Delta q_m = 0$$

where there are i goods in the economy, each with a relevant price, p. In any given period an individual either plans to keep his stock of goods unchanged or plans to increase or decrease his stocks of all or some goods. If Δq is positive he has a planned excess demand, if negative a planned negative excess demand, or, what is the same thing, a planned excess supply. In addition to the i goods there is the further commodity, m, or money with a price of unity. Δq_m can also be positive, negative or zero. Finally, since he is neither thief nor philanthropist, the positive Δqs times their respective ps must equal the negative Δqs times their ps. Sources of funds must equal uses of funds. So if there is as much as one planned excess demand there must be a corresponding planned excess supply to enable the equation to sum to zero. The goods can range from cars to labour to TV sets or to bonds (i.e. the borrowing or lending of money by the sale or purchase of IOUs or certificates of indebtedness).

Now suppose there are K transactors in the economy then a similar equation could be set up for each as in Table 2.1. Since the sum of each row is zero, the sum of the final column is zero—that is Say's Law. The sum of all planned market excess demands, over all

Table 2.1

		Good 1		Good 2			Good i	Money	Sum
Transactor	1	$p_1 \Delta q_{1.1}$	+	$p_2 \Delta q_{2.1}$	$\ldots$	+	$p_i \Delta q_{i.1}$	$+ \Delta q_{m.1}$	$= 0$
Transactor	2	$p_1 \Delta q_{1.2}$	+	$p_2 \Delta q_{2.2}$	$\ldots$	+	$p_i \Delta q_{i.2}$	$+ \Delta q_{m.2}$	$= 0$
$\ldots$		$\ldots$		$\ldots$		$\ldots$	$\ldots$	$\ldots$	$\ldots$
$\ldots$		$\ldots$		$\ldots$		$\ldots$	$\ldots$	$\ldots$	$\ldots$
$\ldots$		$\ldots$		$\ldots$		$\ldots$	$\ldots$	$\ldots$	$\ldots$
Transactor	K	$p_1 \Delta q_1 K$	+	$p_2 \Delta q_2 K$	$\ldots$	+	$p_i \Delta q^i K$	$+ \Delta q_m K$	$= 0$

Planned market excess demands	$P_1 Q_1$	+	$P_2 Q_2$	+	$\ldots$	+	$P_i Q_i$	+	Q_m	$= 0$

goods, including money, is zero. It is not the flip slogan 'supply creates its own demand'. For that to be true each column would add to zero. But if we add transactor 1's planned excess demand for good 1 to transactor 2's down to transactor K's a figure of P_1Q_1 will be arrived at. P_1Q_1 could be positive, negative or zero, as could P_2Q_2 and so on. No single market's planned excess demand need necessarily sum to zero.

Say's Law holds no matter what the price. The table must sum to zero irrespective of the levels of P_1 to P_i. In the special case where each and every market is in equilibrium then no planned excess demand exists anywhere. This, however, only holds for one particular series of prices and is the special case known as general equilibrium (GE). Say's Law holds in GE, but it holds at all other price combinations as well. In GE the prices ruling are such that each column sums to zero. When GE does not hold, Say's Law states that if one market has a price above the GE level, then planned negative excess demand in that market exists. In which case, in at least one other market, the price must be below the GE level for there to be a compensating planned excess demand.

In the ordinary case the price of the good in the market for which there is a planned excess supply would fall, and that of the good for which there is a planned excess demand would rise. GE would be restored and all plans would again be carried out. Economies do not always return to GE, however.

Plans are not always carried out even when they exist, and Say's Law applies only to planned activities. Table 2.2 highlights the difference between planned and effective demands. The four markets normally dealt with in macroeconomics are detailed there.

Stage 1 represents general equilibrium. Total planned excess demand (E_D) in each market is zero. Stage 2 occurs if for some reason the money supply is cut and households find that the average amount of money they hold is less than they would wish or plan to. They respond by curtailing expenditures on commodities in an attempt to build up their money balances. Firms, consequently, sell less than they plan to. Stage 3 occurs as firms react to the fact that unsold stocks of commodities are accumulating and so lay off labour in order to carry out their plans to sell what they actually produce. Stage 4A is arrived at when the price of commodities falls as firms eventually adjust their prices towards the level implied by the fall in demand in the move from stages 1 to 2. (Prices are rarely the first

Table 2.2

	Labour	Commodities	Bonds	Money	Total
Stage 1	0	0	0	0	0
Stage 2	0	E_S	0	E_D	0
Stage 3	E_S	0	0	E_D	0
Stage 4A	E_S	E_D	0	0	0
Stage 4B	E_S	0	0	0	< 0
Stage 4C	E_S	0	0	(E_D)	(0)
Stage 4D	E_S	(E_D)	0	0	(0)

Based on (1) C.W. Baird, *Elements of Macroeconomics*, West 1977 and (2) Axel Leijonhufvud, *Keynes and the Classics*, Institute of Economic Affairs 1969.

economic variables to change. Information is not free and it takes much time and effort before firms determine the optimal response to changing supply and demand conditions.) The system could move from 4A back to stage 1 by a bidding down of wages and a bidding up of commodity prices until the price vector is found where all activities and plans are perfectly coordinated.

In a monetary economy this does not happen in major depressions. The economy has moved out of what Leijonhufvud called 'the corridor' where the normal readjustment process would occur. There is no upward pressure on commodity prices. The offer of labour services (by the unemployed) does not constitute *effective* demand. Stage 4B shows how effective demands can sum to less than zero. Stage 4C and 4D, however, illustrate how Say's principle is still not violated. The sum of *planned* demands is zero. Workers offer their labour services but, since they are not philanthropists, they *plan* to exchange these services for money (4C) or (indirectly) for money and so for goods (4D). The letters in parentheses indicate planned demands which cannot be put into effect.

According to Leijonhufvud (Baird, 1977, p59) this was Keynes' great contribution—namely, the identification of the problem of *effective demand failure*. Moreover, it *could only happen in a monetary economy*, not a barter economy. Workers say to employers, 'We will buy your commodities, but first you must employ us and provide us with the money to make the purchases'. Employers say to workers,

'We will take you on but first you must buy our products in order to provide us with the monetary wherewithal to pay you'. In a barter economy, the problem of the monetary linkage would not be present.

In short, Say's Law is not violated in Stage 4B which refers to effective, not planned, supply and demand. Stage 4B refers only to offers of trade actually made. No offers to buy commodities are made although offers to sell labour (unemployment queues) are present. The plans to buy commodities are present, however, in Stage 4A. But these plans can only be carried out if the money is available. In 4C or 4D the plans cannot be put into effect for just this reason: shortage of money.

So Keynes emphasised the validity of Say's Law that the sum of planned excess demands equals zero. But he also showed how the sum of effective demands can be negative, thus negating the slogan that 'supply creates its own demand'. Effective demands can sum to less than zero because of the uniqueness of money which enters into every transaction, and because of the inflexibility of prices relative to quantity changes.

THE KEYNESIAN REVOLUTION

Keynes undoubtedly had the greatest impact of any economist on government policy in the 1945–70 period. What was the nature of that impact? Two commonly regarded aspects of the Keynesian episode have already been suggested to be untrue. Before proceeding further we will finally dispense with these. First, Keynes allegedly refuted Say's Law and second, and consequentially money was regarded by many of Keynes' followers as relatively unimportant. In the previous pages we argued the reverse; why have some writers suggested otherwise?

Keynes (1960, p18) certainly stated that Say taught that 'supply creates its own demand'. He expanded by quoting from Mill as follows: 'What constitutes the means of payment for commodities is simply commodities'. Unfortunately some interpreters of Keynes drew the conclusions we have already mentioned. In fact, as we have shown, and as Mill (1844) himself stated money is not only important but prices can be sticky and demand can effectively fail (points made by both Keynes and Mill). Mill writes as follows:

There can never, it is said, be a want of buyers for all commodities; because whoever offers a commodity for sale, desires to obtain a commodity in exchange for it . . . sellers and buyers, for all commodities taken together, must . . . be an exact equipoise to each other. . . . This argument is evidently founded on the supposition of a state of barter; and on that supposition . . . the impossibility of an excess of all commodities . . . is perfectly incontestable . . . If, however, we suppose that money is used . . . he who sells . . . needs not buy at the same moment . . . and he does not therefore add to the *immediate* demand for one commodity when he adds to the supply of another . . . For when there is a general anxiety to sell, and a general disinclination to buy, commodities of all kinds remain for a long time unsold, and those which find an immediate market do so at a very low price. If it be said . . . mere money price is not material [but relative values are] . . . we answer this would be true if the low prices were to last . . . But . . . prices will rise again sooner or later [and] the person who is obliged by necessity to sell . . . at a low money price is [thus] really a sufferer . . . Every person, therefore, delays selling if he can . . . There is stagnation to those who are not obliged to sell, and distress to those who are.

So the quantity theory of money developed and popularised by Irving Fisher in the early twentieth century was not debunked (as is sometimes said) by Keynes. The equation or equality $MV \equiv PT$, money multiplied by velocity is equivalent to prices multiplied by the volume of transactions still stood. And Keynes did not deny this. What Keynes found hard to swallow were the inferences of his fellow economists that V was highly stable. On page 296 of *The General Theory* Keynes (1960) *defines* the theory of prices as 'the analysis of the relation between changes in the quantity of money and changes in the price level'. He precedes this remark on the same page by enunciating the quantity theory of money as follows:

So long as there is unemployment, *employment* (or T; emphasis in original) will change in the same proportion as the quantity of money; and when there is full employment, *prices* (emphasis in original) will change in the same proportion as the quantity of money.

In short, velocity or V, could, under certain circumstances, be regarded as a variable which would accommodate itself to changes in M.

A close reading of Keynes, even of the brief selective quotations presented here, nowhere suggests that velocity is being ignored. The early followers of Keynes, however, did regard velocity as a will o' the wisp which would automatically fall by the same percentage as M rose. Any new money would simply be caught in the 'liquidity trap'. And V would take on whatever value was required for $PT \equiv MV$ to hold. They also believed, partly as a consequence, that investment spending would be chronically weak and so government deficit spending would have to be persistently employed to keep aggregate demand at the full employment level. Robertson (1967, pp386–8) commenting on this position of Keynes' early disciples regarding the liquidity trap noted that Keynes himself nowhere argued that liquidity preference was so important. And moreover Keynes denied that it ever had been. 'All this makes it difficult to be sure just what is being asserted' (Robertson, 1967, p388).

Orthodox Keynesianism then developed to the point where the conventional wisdom of the 1950s to early 1970s was that increases in total spending (whether spontaneous or brought about by fiscal or monetary policy) had their main impact on output and employment. Little if anything was said about the price level. Partly this was due to Keynes himself. He argued that wages are inflexible downwards because workers suffer from 'money illusion'. They bargain for and react to changes in their money wages since they have no notion of whether their 'real' wages (i.e. their money wages in relation to other money prices) are rising or falling. Firms thus lay off workers rather than cut wages in a recession; or workers choose to be laid off rather than accept a money wage cut.

In an era when most trades unions employ resident economists and the rate of inflation is announced in the mass media with monthly regularity at the least, one is inclined to be slightly sceptical of Keynes' belief that all of the workers can be fooled all of the time. More importantly, in his Chapter on Money Wages, Keynes (1960, p269) makes some remarks which are startling in their apparent internal inconsistency. He states:

[to] suppose a flexible wage-policy is a right and proper adjunct of a system which on the whole is one of *laissez-faire* is the opposite of the truth. It is only in a highly authoritarian society . . . that a flexible wage-policy could function with success. One can imagine it in operation in Italy, Germany or Russia, but not in France, the United States or Great Britain.

Because of this implication that free markets mean inflexibility and authoritarianism permits rapid market adjustments it is then not surprising to discover that in the 1937 Preface to the German edition of *The General Theory* Keynes wrote:

The theory of aggregate production . . . that is the goal of the following book can be much more easily applied to conditions of a totalitarian state than the theory of the production and distribution of a given output turned out under the conditions of free competition and of a considerable degree of *laissez-faire*.

Let us now tie these threads together. Government action was seen by Keynesians (and approved by Keynes) as a harbinger of general full employment equilibrium. The velocity of money was perceived to be an accommodating will o' the wisp. Workers would be willing to continue working for lower real wages brought about by rising money prices. Changes in the general price level could, therefore, be ignored, or if they became a problem at full employment levels could be tackled by institutional means such as incomes policies. This latter view being based on the notion that most price increases are determined by costs, and in particular by 'excessive' wage demands.

The Keynesian revolution did not radically depart from the Marshallian scheme of things in its methodology (the equilibrium of the Keynesian cross: the intersection of the $C + I + G$ line and the 45° line of elementary texts is not conceptually dissimilar to Marshall's supply and demand curves). Rather the main break was at the level of aggregation. The Marshallian cross can be applied to each market. Contrariwise the Keynesian cross is only applicable when plotting aggregate demand or expenditures against aggregate supply or national income. Aggregates are moved to centre stage. In addition whereas the quantity equivalence of exchange ($PT \equiv MT$) emphasised money and the price level, Keynesians focussed on output, incomes and employment.

THE PHILLIPS CURVE

When rises in the average price level came to be perceived as a problem in the late 1950s and early 1960s Professor A W Phillips produced the results of an empirical study carried out on wage rates and unemployment in Britain from 1862 to 1957. The relationship he discovered, now known as the Phillips curve, was declared by

Professor Paul Samuelson (Nobel Prizewinner, and a leading Keynesian) to be 'one of the most important concepts of our times' (cited in Bell, 1981, p66). The connection as empirically discovered by Phillips and theoretically refined by many later writers suggested a policy trade-off was possible between unemployment and inflation. Since it used nominal, not real values, it fitted easily into the Keynesian scenario of 'money illusion'. Either monetary or fiscal policy could be used to increase or decrease the rate of inflation which in turn would be followed respectively by a rise in employment or unemployment. Unfortunately the simple Phillips curve barely survived the next decade of either theoretical investigation or empirical experience. Inflation and unemployment both continued to increase thus challenging the relationship's validity. While writers such as Friedman argued (for example in his 1968 Presidential Address to the American Economic Association) that any trade-off which existed must be between unemployment and un-anticipated inflation. That is workers cannot forever be tricked into accepting a lower share of national income because of money illusion. If a government temporarily succeeds in reducing employment by increasing inflation money illusion will shortly vanish and only if the inflation rate is increased still further can unemployment be held down yet again. Thus an ever-accelerating inflation rate is required to hold unemployment at any given level since inflationary expectations will continuously catch up with actuality. In this scenario the traditional Phillips curve is a short-run or even transient phenomenon whose position continuously shifts dependent on the state of inflationary expectations. The line these short-run (expectations augmented) curves traces given the relevant observed coordinates at points in time has become known as the long-run Phillips curve. At its simplest the long-run curve is close to a vertical line indicating stable unemployment which, if above the 'natural' rate can only be maintained there at a socially impossible explosive rate of inflation.

Keynesianism, even after this skin-graft of the Phillips curve, has thus proven unequal to the task of either explaining or managing the economy. Keynes himself did not reject the importance of money, nor did he argue that markets cannot adjust unaided (unless there is effective demand failure). He did, however, argue for the existence of money illusion. And there he was at odds with the original quantity theorists who argued that people would attempt to maintain the same level of real money balances or purchasing power. Thus if the relation between nominal and real balances changed, say due to inflation, then people would increase their nominal balances to reattain the desired level of real balances. Thus although Keynes agreed with the quantity theorists that wages were sticky downwards (Bell, 1981, p66) he disagreed that as a consequence labour lay-offs, unemployment and a resulting general fall in the price level would bring about a spontaneous increase in spending from the increased value of real money balances. Rather he feared the economy would enter the Leijonhufvudian corridor of effective demand failure.

The macroeconomic 'advances' of several decades seem then to have failed to increase our understanding or to draw theory and practice closer together. Keynes himself seemed to recognise this. In a written reply to some critiques of *The General Theory* (cited in Bell, 1981, p65) he gave a retort which was nearly, if not quite, that of an Austrian economist. Unemployment and general economic instability he attributed to the inherent uncertainty of knowledge, the inability to know in advance the consequences of actions, the impossibility of making forecasts or consequently of knowing what capital returns might be. 'About these matters,' wrote Keynes, 'there is no scientific basis on which to form any calculable probability whatever. *We simply do not know.*' (emphasis added).

MONOPOLISTIC COMPETITION

If macroeconomics became divorced from reality and the attempts of the Quantity Theorists, Keynes and Phillips failed to stop the drift then microeconomics was in no better shape. The concept of Pareto optimality has already been noted as has Lord Robbins' definition of economics (p10).

Paretian optimality, however, although logically elegant requires economic modelling based on the theory and assumptions of what had come to be known as perfect competition. The requirements of perfect knowledge by a multiplicity of buyers and sellers, none of whom is large enough to influence market price by withholding supply or custom, product homogeneity, easy market entry and exit are the conditions for the well known equilibrium situation of $P = MC = $ minimum AC. The assumptions are of course totally unrealistic, although that in itself is insufficient to damn perfect competition. (A more relevant Austrian style complaint would be that *knowledge is a consequence not a condition of competition*.) Nonetheless we noted (p9) that economics as a discipline was subject to such criticisms, and the rarefied concept of perfect competition was held as no exception to the feeling that economics was unhelpful either for aiding general understanding or for policy making.

Monopoly, of course, was understood to be the opposite and limiting case. And Marshall (1966, p410) even recognised the existence of 'monopolistic cartels'. Nonetheless although this latter concept was included in his chapter on 'The Theory of Monopoly', the chapter itself occupied only 16 pages. His emphasis, like that of the perfect competition literature was on the price and output decisions of the monopolist. Only if the monopolist wished to increase consumers' surplus (for example in order to grow in the long run) would he charge a lower price than the full profit maximising one (Marshall, pp402–5). Even in a chapter of that brevity Marshall was concerned with productive efficiency in the monopoly (or cartel). This, of course, was in the tradition of the perfect competition literature where the industry structure and theoretical assumptions ensured that each firm did produce at the most efficient level (i.e. at the foot of a U-shaped AC curve).

It was Edward Chamberlin who made the greatest non-Austrian attempt to bring theory closer to reality with his book *The Economics of Monopolistic Competition* (1933). The Chamberlinian 'tangency solution' retained equilibrium as an outcome of analysis. However that solution did not result in productive (foot of the AC curve) efficiency. Chamberlin's big point of departure was his movement away from exclusive emphasis on price and output decisions to product oriented decisions. Product homogeneity was not assumed. Firms could, by product differentiation, branding and similar marketing activities obtain a downward sloping demand curve for their product. Prices are set neither at minimum AC nor at marginal cost. Pareto optimality and productive efficiency thus both disappear and the situation is open to charges of 'waste' in a way that perfect competition is not. Chamberlin (1950) in a much later article tried to close the Pandora's box which he had apparently opened. Since most industries were neither monopolistic nor perfectly competitive business generally came under attack as being insensitive to consumer wants. The invisible hand and consumer sovereignty seemed to be concepts belonging to some fictitious golden age. But argued Chamberlin, surely *increased knowledge of consumer wants*

24

could well raise the level of product differentiation in a market? To meet variegated consumer wants is surely not socially undesirable? But Chamberlin's plea that the activity of the discovery of knowledge is important (like Keynes' belated emphasis on ignorance), although possessing a strong Austrian emphasis, was ignored. For the four decades after his *magnum opus* economics at the level of the industry and the firm developed what is now known as the Structure: Conduct: Performance paradigm (S:P:C). A fuller critique of the S:C:P paradigm was given in the present writer's *Industry, Prices and Markets* (1979) where both the empirical and theoretical under-pinnings were discussed in some detail. In essence the model argues that perfect competition is 'good' and the more concentrated markets become the less socially desirable are their Conduct and Performance, particularly when assessed against the yardstick of pricing at marginal cost. As a consequence Richard Nelson was able to say in a *Bell Journal* review article in 1976 that '[i]industrial organisation is a field that is in deep intellectual trouble. The source of that trouble is that old textbook theory that we all know so well.'

Thus Chamberlin and his successors, like their colleagues in macroeconomics were engaged in refining and perfecting the conceptual tools for analysing the relevant equilibria. Knowledge, information and ignorance were given passing obeisance but were never placed in centre stage. Most economists, in fact, ignored the problem of knowledge. This the Austrians refused to do (and in the 1930s and 1940s this applied particularly to Hayek) and as a consequence they too tended to be unacknowledged. Had the profession been aware of this then it might not now be undergoing the painful trauma of rewriting, rediscovering and reformulating many of the premises and 'advances' of the last six decades.

None of these four attempts to link theory with reality have proven successful in Austrian eyes. (The Quantity Theory of Money, Keynesianism, the Phillips Curve and Monopolistic Competition). The next two chapters deal, at a micro and a macro level respectively, with some of the criticisms Austrians were making of the economic orthodoxy as it developed from Marshall through Keynes and Chamberlin to the 1960s. This then leads into the second half of the book where some aspects of modern day Austrianism are examined in detail.

REFERENCES

C W Baird, *Elements of Macroeconomics*, West, 1977.
D Bell, 'Models and Reality in Economic Discourse' in *The Crisis in Economic Theory*, D Bell and I Kristol (eds), Basic Books, 1981.
E H Chamberlin, 'Product Heterogeneity and Public Policy' *American Economic Review*, 1950.
J M Keynes, *The General Theory of Employment, Interest and Money*, Macmillan, 1960.
J S Mill, 'On the Influence of Consumption on Production' from *Essays on Some Unsettled Questions of Political Economy*, 1844.
I Kirzner, 'The Austrian Perspective on the Crisis' in Bell and Kristol *op. cit.*
A Marshall, *Principles of Economics*, 8th edition, Macmillan, 1966.
L Robbins, *The Nature and Significance of Economic Science*, Macmillan, 1935.
D S Robertson, *Lectures on Economic Principles*, Fontana, 1967.
A Smith, *The Wealth of Nations*, A Skinner (ed), Pelican, 1976.

3 The Austrian Response at a Micro level

To understand why Austrian economists reject the neo-classical advances in the equilibrium theory of monopolistic competition and the like it is first necessary to comprehend Austrian methodology. This in turn provides an explanation of why mathematical economics has been rejected by Austrians and why econometrics has been relegated by them from the eminent position of a tester of theories to a technological tool. In this chapter we examine the method and goals of Austrian economics, the nature of exchange in a non-equilibrium society and the distinctive role of knowledge in a world of imperfect information.

A SCIENCE OF HUMAN ACTION

Praxeology, or the science of human action, defined at its simplest is the careful following through, by verbal deductive reasoning, of the logical implications of a small number of self-evident truths about human behaviour. The principal and original axiom on which Austrianism rests is that of *purposive* action. Individuals consciously act in order to achieve chosen goals. Mises (1976, p34) puts it this way:

The characteristic feature of man is action. Man aims at changing some of the conditions of his environment in order to substitute a state of affairs that suits him better for another state that suits him less . . . Action is purposive conduct. It is not simply behaviour, but behaviour begot by judgments of value, aiming at a definite end and guided by ideas concerning the suitability or unsuitability of definite means.

The axiom that man acts does *not* mean that man is a rational actor in the neoclassical sense. To use the wording of neo-classical texts when they discuss indifference analysis: it is *not* assumed that man has not passed the satiation rate of consumption; is totally knowledgeable about the range of choices confronting him; that tastes are given; that he has consistency and transitivity between his preferences; and that time and taste changes are exogenous to the discussion. (A similar negation of the claim that 'purposive'equals 'rational' could be made using wording applicable to the neo-classical production function and technical change.)

That the very first and fundamental axiom requires this exposition and elaboration is unfortunate but unavoidable. As recently as 1981 (p2) no less an economist than Lord Robbins appeared to misunderstand it. Robbins remarked:

. . . our explanations must to some extent be *teleological*. This is not to argue with von Mises and some of his followers that we must regard human action, if not purely vegetative, as at all times *rational* in the sense that, given belief in the range of technical knowledge available to individuals or collections of individuals action must be *consistent*. I confess that I have never been able to understand this contention . . . (emphasis in original).

The point at issue is resolved when one sees that Robbins and Mises are defining the word 'rational' differently. Rothbard (1976, p19) points out that all Misesian action is rational in the sense that it is *not* 'purely *reflexive*, or knee-jerk, behaviour which is not directed towards goals' (emphasis in original).

If individuals act purposively (and Austrians take this as a self-evident truth) then other axioms follow. The individual actor must have chosen certain goals which, if achieved, he believes will leave him better off in some way which is valuable to him. In acting he must employ means which he believes will help him achieve the desired ends. Individuals need not have identical tastes and values, and they need not have identical technological know-how. Praxeology makes no judgements as to whether the individual's value scale is 'right' in any moral or welfare sense, nor whether his chosen means will in fact attain his desired ends. 'All that praxeology asserts is that the individual actor adopts goals and believes, whether erroneously or correctly, that he can arrive at them by the employment of certain means' (Rothbard, 1976, p20).

Further axioms are that all human beings differ in tastes and abilities, and all action takes place through time. An action takes place now (and/or in the immediate future) and is directed towards an end or state of affairs which does not currently exist. (If the state of affairs *did* exist in the present there would be no need for action.) Moreover since action takes place through time and the future is never known with complete certainty then actions may produce unexpected outcomes for the actor. People will learn from such (pleasant or unpleasant) experiences and their revealed errors will cause them to alter their actions in the future. By implication, then, Robbinsian rationality and consistency in choice of ends and means cannot fit into this praxeological schema.

The foundations of praxeology are held to be universally true and epistemologically empirical. Not empirical in the sense of physical science research since if they are true, they cannot be verified by continued failure to falsify the hypotheses they give rise to. Nor are they empirical in the sense that they can be tested by historical or statistical means. First, there is no need for such testing (since they *are* true if the logic used in their development is correct). And second, historical and statistical data only aid in determining which axioms to apply in any given case (since no two cases are identical). The empiricism which is appropriate to praxeology is Aristotelian. A proposition which is logically false is one which does not correspond with empirical reality. Rothbard (1976, p27) and Kirzner (1976, pp62–3) both agree that only the initiating axiom of purposive action is *a priori* or 'introspective'. The subsidiary axioms are 'broadly empirical' and rest not on introspection, but rather their deduced truth 'depends on our observations of our fellow men'.

We have already seen (p5) how Austrianism can be traced back to Aristotelian philosophy in the area of subjective utility. This is also true with regard to praxeology. Aristotle, in the first book of the *Physica* distinguished between 'matter' (the substratum that perseveres in the phenomenon of change) and 'form' (the active principle that defines the nature of the product of change). Mises argues that the scope of praxeology is:

. . . human action as such, irrespective of all environmental, accidental, and individual circumstances of the concrete acts. Its cognition is purely formal and general without reference to the material content and the particular features of the actual case. It aims at knowledge valid for all instances in which the conditions exactly correspond to those implied in its assumptions and inferences.

Praxeology seeks out the essence or 'form' in human action, not the particular or specific case. It is history which deals with 'matter' or individual events. To explain such events the historian calls on the 'knowledge provided by (all the theoretical sciences) . . . but especially by praxeology' (Mises, 1966, p49). Theory precedes history.

POSITIVE ECONOMICS AND PRAXEOLOGY

Economists of the Chicago School hold a *prima facie* similar stance. They have a greater faith in theory than most other non-Austrians (*pace* their application of theory to many neglected areas of economic activity from marriage to theft). As a consequence, because of their methodological orientation, they engage in a broader range of empirical investigations than do many other economists. As in praxeology, theory precedes empiricism (but there the resemblance ends) and provided the theory is not refuted it is regarded as 'explaining' the facts. As Friedman put it (1974, p15) 'the relevant question to ask about the theory is not whether [it is] . . . descriptively "realistic" . . . but whether [it is] sufficiently good . . . for the purpose in hand.' Friedman's billiard player (1974, p21) illustrates this argument:

Consider the problem of predicting the shots made by an expert billiard player. It seems not at all unreasonable that excellent predictions would be yielded by the hypothesis that the billiard player made his shots as if he knew the complicated mathematical formulae that would give the optimum directions of travel, could estimate accurately by eye the angles, etc, describing the location of the balls, could make lightning calculations from the formulae, and could then make the balls travel in the direction indicated by the formulae. Our confidence in this hypothesis is not based on the belief that billiard players, even expert ones, can or do go through the process described; it derives rather from the belief that unless in some way or other they were capable of reaching essentially the same result, they would not in fact be expert billiard players.

It may appear that the positive economists adopt the view that theory in the physical sciences, in positivism and in praxeology has the same objective. In each theorising aims at identifying 'form', that which is universal and essential. But this is not so. The physicist does:

he can actually examine the 'matter' of a situation. He can and does identify the nature and properties of the billiard balls, cues and table and then formulates predictable mathematical propositions. Kirkpatrick (1983, p45) argues that he 'can abstract the "form" of a situation from any time or space constraints . . . with a mathematical precision that is repeatable and invariant from time to time and place to place, given the same conditions.'

In positive economics, however, the theory is no more than a 'tentative guess' (Kirzner, 1967, p106) awaiting confirmation by the evidence and resting on the 'as if' postulate. If the theory works, that is if it appears to explain events satisfactorily then it is acceptable (until refuted or until a superior theory in terms of explanatory power and/or ease of use is 'tentatively guessed' at). Predictability not the identification of universal and essential 'form' is the goal of positivist theorising.

This is the aim of praxeology, however. But since historical facts, although sometimes similar are always heterogeneous, empirical work has 'the function of establishing the *applicability* of particular theorems, and thus *illustrating* their operation' (Kirzner 1967, p107) (emphasis in original). Confirmation of theory is not possible because there are no constants in human action, nor is it necessary because the theorems themselves describe relationships logically developed from hypothesised conditions. Failure of a logically derived axiom to fit the facts does not render it invalid, rather it 'might merely indicate inapplicability' to the circumstances of the case (Kirzner, 1967, p107).

Praxeologists can measure historical facts but do not claim they lead to accurate predictions simply because historical events among the actions of men are unique and unrepeatable. Econometricians are not theorists but historians. Relationships between human actions are never constant because of the axioms of consciousness and free will. Economic phenomena, such as a rise in supply and corresponding fall in price, are the results of such human actions. The actions may be consequent on a decline in the intensity of some consumers' wants for a given good and/or an increase in the desire of some producers to supply the same product. A historical elasticity of demand or supply can be computed *ceteris paribus* since these actions occurred at a certain point in time and space. But other things will never be equal again. The praxeological axioms preclude mathematical prediction.

The essence of the law of supply and demand is that it states what must happen: it does not state what usually happens; it is accurate and irrefutable but it is not precise (Mises, 1966, pp54–6 and 350–7). Since any individual can at any moment change his plan of action the quantifiable phenomena of markets such as prices, costs, quantities and numbers of consumers are in perpetual flux. The actor can only cope with this uncertainty by speculation. '[A]ction necessarily always aims at future and therefore uncertain conditions and thus is always speculation. Acting man looks, as it were, with the eyes of a historian into the future' (Mises, 1966, p58). The physical scientist, on the other hand, can predict with near certainty, given known constraints, that a solid object will fall to the ground at a specific and accelerating rate. The relations are constant. Among men they are not. On this view, the positivist who tests his theories 'as if' the relations were constant is both misguided and in error.

QUANTITATIVE ECONOMICS AND ECONOMETRICS

Where then does this leave mathematical economics and econometrics? Karl Menger (1973, p43), the mathematician son of Carl Menger, argued that mathematical discussion is no more precise than verbal reasoning, but suffers from being less general. He considered the sentence that for '*a higher price of a good there corresponds a lower (or at any rate not a higher)*' quantity demanded. This he denoted by (2) and as (2') the following: '*If p denotes the price of, and q the (quantity demanded of) a good then* $q = f(p)$ *and* $dq/dp = f'(p) \leqslant 0$.' He continued:

[those] who regard the formula (2') as more precise or more mathematical than sentence (2) are under a complete misapprehension . . . The only difference between (2) and (2') is this: since (2') is limited to functions which are differentiable and whose graphs have tangents (which from an economic point of view are not more plausible than curvature) the sentence (2) is *more general*, but it is by no means less precise: *it is of the same mathematical precision as (2')*. (emphasis in original).

To be sure mathematical economists have now progressed beyond the differential and integral calculus, the disadvantages of which are laid out above. More important than the discontinuities and irregularities of relationships which the calculus cannot handle (but which other techniques such as set theory can) is the Austrian emphasis on the study of the competitive process *through time*. The nature of changes in time, their degree and intensity, and even their direction cannot be deduced from initial axioms. If they could then mathematical economics would be of value as a concise reasoning tool. But human action is not 'preprogrammed'. Learning occurs, tastes and technologies change, exogenous variables are continuously imparting new shocks to the system. Only if these variables could be perfectly foreseen would mathematics be of value for conciseness. Since they are not, even if they were tractable by mathematics, the symbols and their relationships would have to be continuously respecified. Egger (1978, p30) argues that this never ending require-ment for redefinition and respecification of any mathematical model renders mathematics cumbersome and inefficient (the major strengths of the science in other areas) for use as a praxeological tool. It is the presence of time and uncertainty that makes mathematics of little value to Austrians rather than its inability to handle their economic data. And time and uncertainty, learning and expectation revisions are elements which are inherent in human action but which cannot concisely be treated by abstract mathematical symbolism before, and during the ever changing events.

Econometricians, however, do have a role to play in Austrian economics. Econometrics is viewed as a useful tool which can be *one* aid to the interpretation of economic history. It can be *one* tool for the businessman seeking advice on alternative strategies *given known current conditions*. But neither the observer, the businessman, nor the econometrician should imagine that the tool itself can discover economic laws in advance. To cite Rizzo (1978, p53), for 'while man necessarily acts, it does not follow that he *always* acts, i.e. that he *never* engages in automatic response to stimuli or some kind of nonpurposive behaviour.'

KNOWLEDGE, PLANNING AND TIME

If there are 'no constraints' where then does praxeology lead us? Lord Robbins (1935, p16) is widely quoted as saying that economics 'is the science which studies human behaviour as a relationship between ends and means which have alternative uses'. This is at once misleading, incomplete and imprecise. Where ends and means are given (as is implicit in this definition), resource allocation *per se* is a problem which can be solved by pure mathematical logic. All that is required is that the marginal rates of substitution between any two commodities or factors be the same in all their different uses. Study of the competitive process is thus unnecessary and optimal allocation can be obtained either by the achievement of equilibrium in a perfectly competitive market or by the calculations of an omni-competent mind. The problem is then purely technological, not economic or praxeological.

The economic problem, however, is not how the most efficient allocation of given resources can be achieved in order to best attain known goals. Rather, as Hayek (1945) argues, it is concerned with 'how to secure the best use of resources known to any of the members of the society, for ends whose relative importance only these individuals know'. The relevant framework is not one of given ends and given means. It is a matter of generating sufficient information to permit and encourage willing buyers and sellers to maximise the net gains which would accrue to them through the process of exchange.

Economics is concerned with choice in the presence of uncertainty. If we assume (realistically) the absence of an omnicompetent mind and (desirably) the lack of coercion in society, then a study of industrial organisation can help us to understand how the problem is solved. A perfectly competitive market structure in equilibrium is not the answer. What is required is an understanding of why people act, decide, and choose in the way they do in the presence of uncertainty and the absence of 'constants' about the consequences of their actions.

How can efficient use of knowledge (itself a scarce commodity) be ensured?

To the economist each individual has a large store of two types of private knowledge. First there are preferences, particularly consumer preferences. A consumer's preferences are generally unknown to others until he discloses them by choosing one product against another. Similarly, a worker's job preferences are revealed when he pursues a particular occupation. Preferences are private knowledge until actions reveal them.

Second, there is the knowledge of being in a unique situation: the knowledge of the 'man on the spot'. For instance, the manager of an electric showroom and repair shop knows his workers' skills, their personalities, how well they get on with each other, where to hire part-time labour, which equipment is in good condition, which is likely to need repair, where to get spare parts, where to get stock if supplies are interrupted, when business is likely to be busy and when slack, his customers' particular needs, and so on. This is essentially private knowledge since the manager is in a unique location, dealing with unique individuals, servicing and using unique equipment and the like. Clearly, production decisions must somehow take the unique knowledge of this and other such 'men on the spot' into account.

But efficiency requires more than that production decisions be based on private knowledge. There must exist a means by which each producer's decisions tend to co-ordinate with the decisions of all the other producers and consumers in the market. On the face of it, this appears impossible. How is an individual to co-ordinate his decisions with those of millions of others when their decisions are at least partly based on private knowledge which he does not possess? Private knowledge of the kind described cannot, by its very nature, be conveyed in the statistical aggregates of central or governmental plans. These require data reduction and foreknowledge, both of which are, by definition, precluded from private knowledge. To fully appreciate these problems, we need to consider how production and consumption decisions are co-ordinated.

CO-ORDINATION

Hayek (1945) explains the operation thus:

Fundamentally, in a system in which the knowledge of the relevant facts is dispersed among many people, prices can act to co-ordinate the separate actions of different people . . . It is worth contemplating for a moment a very simple and commonplace instance of the action of the price system to see what precisely it accomplishes. Assume that somewhere in the world a new opportunity for the use of some raw material, say, tin, has arisen, or that one of the sources of supply of tin has been eliminated. It does not matter for our purpose – and it is significant that it does not matter – which of these two causes had made tin more scarce. All that the users of tin need to know is that some of the tin they used to consume is now more profitably employed elsewhere and that, in consequence, they must economise tin. There is no need for the great majority of them even to know where the more urgent need has arisen, or in favour of what other needs they ought to husband the supply. If only some of them know directly of the new demand, and switch resources over to it, and if the people who are aware of the new gap thus created in turn fill it from still other sources, the effect will rapidly spread throughout the whole economic system and influence not only all the uses of tin but also those of its substitutes and the substitutes of these substitutes, the supply of all things made of tin, and their substitutes, and so on; and all this without the great majority of those instrumental in bringing about these substitutions knowing anything at all about the original cause of these changes. The whole acts as one market, not because any of its members survey the whole field, but because their limited individual fields of vision sufficiently overlap so that through many intermediaries the relevant information is communicated to all. The mere fact that there is one price for any commodity—or rather that local prices are connected in a manner determined by the cost of transport, etc—brings about the solution which (it is just conceptually possible) might have been arrived at by one single mind possessing all the information which is in fact dispersed among all the people involved in the process.

The 'solution' referred to is, of course, perfectly competitive equilibrium. Thus it would seem that we have come full circle and returned to the Walrasian or Marshallian model. Not so. Hayek (1937) would be the first to ask why we are concerned with this 'admittedly fictitious state of equilibrium.' His explicit response, implicit above, is that 'the only justification for this is the supposed existence of a tendency towards equilibrium'. The tendency exists because of the information prices convey to entrepreneurs. Differentials between bid and offer prices signal to entrepreneurs that profits are available if by their actions they can narrow the spread. Entrepreneurship is the essence of the competitive process. It is an equilibrating force, moving bid and offer prices closer together.

Because knowledge is divided among millions of individuals with no one knowing more than a tiny part, factors of production are often employed where they make less than the maximum contribution. A producer may be unaware that a factor could make a greater contribution in another employment. Those who know of other employments may be unaware of the availability of the factor.

To correct such misallocations the price system (1) provides a means of discovering resource misdirection, (2) stimulates use of the means of discovery, (3) encourages transfer of resource control to producers who have discovered such misallocations, and (4) rewards their corrections (Summers, 1977).

PROCESS AND EQUILIBRIUM

Suppose, for example, tin is being used to make products on which consumers place low values, and/or it is being used where each ton of tin contributes little to physical output. In these cases, each ton of tin makes only a small contribution to the revenues of the manufacturer using it.

As a result, manufacturers place low values on tin, and it can be obtained for a low price. Now suppose an entrepreneur surveys the situation and discovers what he believes to be a more profitable way of using tin: by making a product which he hopes consumers will value highly and/or by using a method of production which gets more output per unit input. If he is wrong—and has overestimated the prices consumers will pay and/or underestimated his costs—he will fare no better than most other producers and have little impact on the market. If he is right, however, he will soon earn high profits because each ton of tin will make a large contribution to his revenues. His profits will encourage and enable him to expand and he will bid more tin away from other producers. Other firms will notice his profits, stop using tin in the old and relatively unproductive employments, and start copying his use of tin. This will result in competitive bidding raising the price of tin so reflecting its more productive use. Simultaneously, increased output will reduce the price of the entrepreneur's product. Competition ensures that the entrepreneur has no guarantee of permanent profits.

Of course, anyone can look back and assert which producers were the next most successful in using each factor of production where it made the greatest contribution. But no one can look forward, before the fact, and assert which producer will prove to be the most efficient. That has to be decided by the competitive process itself.

In summary, the competitive process provides incentives and so evokes effort. It generates a continuous and universal search for substitutes, for ways of replacing the less desirable by the more desirable. This process of substitution begins with the consumer seeking to distribute his income to the best advantage and passes on to the producer striving to replace the less by the more sought after goods and substituting a better way of producing for a worse way. The essence of the process is choice by the consumer; emulation, rivalry and substitution by the producer.

By competition we ought to mean mobility, not equilibrium. We ought to mean the unbarred movement of factors of production from low reward occupations to high reward ones; the unbarred movement of consumer patronage from high-priced to low-priced suppliers of identical goods. For this to occur *knowledge* that such movement is worthwhile is required. This is the function of the entrepreneur: to seek out such opportunities before others perceive them. Rivalry is of the essence in this process. But rivalry, indeed, as McNulty (1968) points out, even the very verb 'to compete', is precluded from the equilibrium of 'perfect competition'. Any competitive action by a businessman (for example, a price cut) is regarded in pure theory as evidence that he possesses some monopoly power. Yet what kind of market power is it that a 'non-perfectly competitive' businessman has? The power is no more or less than that of the odd-job man who advertises his services in a small town newspaper. He could charge a higher price or a lower price if he so wishes. But if he also wishes to maximise his income or wealth he is constrained by the market to charge the profit maximising price. Such 'monopoly power' is as relevant as the power each of us has to give away our wealth.

The trial and error price cuts or increases made by businessmen are simply examples of ways they attempt to gain information as to where the profit maximising price is. Trial and error price adjustments, advertising decisions, product variations and other forms of rivalry are merely methods of gleaning market information in situations where knowledge is imperfect and costly to obtain.

Some non-Austrian economists have explicitly noted this 'price searching' behaviour but have failed to follow their arguments through to a full praxeological conclusion. For example Arrow in 1959 admitted (p55) that 'perfect competition can really prevail only at equilibrium'. In monopoly (p57) the firm 'presumably does not know the entire demand curve, for otherwise [it] would jump immediately to the optimal position'. Arrow's (1959, p57) use of the word 'presumably' denotes his less than full commitment to the notion of uncertainty and indeed he only admits the '*possibility* of a discrepancy between output and demand for a monopolist' (emphasis added).

Even more interesting are his comments on perfect competition.

The law that there is only one price on a competitive market (Jevons' Law of Indifference) is derived on the basis of profit- or utility-maximising behaviour on the part of both sides of the market; but there is no reason for such behaviour to lead to a unique price except in equilibrium, or possibly under conditions of perfect knowledge (Arrow, 1959, p58).

Arrow explains this by postulating the instance of demand exceeding (a short-run totally inelastic) supply. The firm is faced with a sloping demand curve and will act as a *monopolist* raising his price tentatively until profit maximisation is reached. But other firms will also be doing the same and so his demand curve 'is thus shifting upward at the same time he is exploring it' (p59). '[T]he uncertainty during this process is apt to be very considerable.' Guesses will have to be made about other suppliers' prices, cost conditions and the industry demand as a whole. So the 'whole adjustment process is apt to be very irregular . . . [all of which] . . . puts a premium on information . . .' (p59).

Arrow goes on (1959, p59) that by a 'parallel argument each buyer on a (perfectly competitive, non-equilibrium) market with an inequality between supply and demand *can be regarded as a monopsonist*' (emphasis added). As a consequence price indeterminacy is inherent even in a market populated by 'perfect competitors'. There is no auctioneer: only a collection of monopolists and monopsonists groping for an equilibrium price.

Arrow's arguments help illumine or underline some of the Austrian views on knowledge, planning and time which we have already hinted at. Hayek's 1937 paper, for example, becomes easier to understand. There he argues that equilibrium analysis has meaning only when various actions are related to each other. Thus the notion of an *individual's* equilibrium is of significance in so far as a person's activities can be understood as part of one plan (i.e. his, the individual's). The data possessed by the individual planner may, but need not be, objectively factual. It is sufficient that the individual *believes* them to be so. Any knowledge change in these circumstances will disrupt the equilibrium relationship between actions taken before the actions taken after the alteration in knowledge. The passage of time is thus essential to give meaning to this concept of equilibrium. Even if an individual's plan is based on incorrect assumptions concerning the external facts, there will always be some conceivable and unique set of external events which would make it possible in principle to execute the original plan.

CO-ORDINATING INDEPENDENT PLANS

Hayek stresses, however, that the validity of the equilibrium model ceases to hold good *when we move from the individual to the group*. Here plans are determined simultaneously but independently by a number of different persons. Hayek (1937) points out that if such plans are *all* to be carried out then it is necessary for three conditions to hold.

First, each must be based on the same set of beliefs regarding external events, otherwise if conflicting expectations were held, there would be no unique set of external events which would make it possible to accomplish all of the plans. Second, with mutual exchange, the various plans must be compatible. One person's plan must be built on the data which exactly corresponds to the actions contained by another's. This difficulty is traditionally sidestepped by assuming that the same data (for example prices, tastes, technology) are equally given to all, and that the plans will adapt to each other somehow provided each individual is motivated in a similar manner. This, of course, does not overcome the difficulty, nor avoid the circular reasoning that one person's actions are the other person's data. Third, and this is Hayek's unique contribution, these data assumed given to each individual as objectively factual in group equilibrium differ from the data possessed by the individual in the analysis of individual equilibrium. There subjectivity *was* permitted. We consequently have a major internal inconsistency in the argument.

'Data' has been used with two meanings: as an objective array of facts available to the observer and in a subjective sense as things known to or believed by the individuals whose behaviour we are attempting to explain. To maintain consistency between the analyses of the individual and of society we must use 'data' in the subjective sense in both instances. (Or, alternatively, in the objective sense. But this would imply perfect knowledge by each individual, and no uncertainty.)

Societal equilibria are then possible in two sets of circumstances. Mutual plan compatibility and a given set of external events may permit an equilibrium in which no planner is disappointed. If equilibrium does not exist, however, plan revision by some people what Hayek (1937) called 'endogenous' disturbances, are inevitable

Or, secondly, equilibrium is possible if the subjective and what we have called the objective data correspond. Are the expectations on which plans are based borne out by the facts? If so, an equilibrium will *have* existed but it will only be identifiable at the end of the period planned. Any interim unforeseen developments in objective data (often termed exogenous) would be evidence of a lack of equilibrating correspondence between subjective and objective data. But to speak of such a data change is only meaningful in the unlikely event of initially coinciding expectations: the first type of societal equilibrium must have existed. Had it not, then someone's hopes would have been fulfilled or disappointed by the change in external facts, and there would then 'be no possibility of deciding what was a change in the objective data'.

As a consequence, Hayek (1937) points out that societal equilibrium (unlike that of a person) *can* be spoken of as a static, point in time, phenomenon. However, it merely means mutually compatible action plans. It will continue only so long as the common expectations of all individuals correspond to the external data. But it need not be confined to a stationary situation. Provided that data changes have similar and simultaneous impacts on individual expectations and do not alter the compatibility requirement, equilibrium analysis becomes applicable to dynamic processes. (At this point Hayek inserts a footnote indicating that 'this separation of the concept of equilibrium from that of a stationary state' is logically 'necessary' and began 'with Marshall and his distinction between long- and short-run equilibriums'.)

Thus on the relationship between equilibrium and foresight, equilibrium means that everyone's foresight with regard to each other's actions, with regard to the same set of external facts is correct. Correct foresight is more than a necessary condition, it is a sufficient condition for equilibrium. Equilibrium will last for as long as anticipations are correct, and anticipations need only be correct on points relating to the decisions of individuals.

It follows that equilibrium cannot be deduced either from objective data (since analysis of what people will do can start only from what is *known to them*) or from one person's or group of persons' subjective data (since differing subjective data would already determine whether or not equilibrium exists, ie whether or not compatibility of plans exists). Hayek (1937) then, having demolished the possibility of *identifying* equilibrium, asserts (p36 above) that the tendency towards it is the main reason for concern with it.

That is, *under certain conditions* the knowledge and intentions of different society members move into agreement; and their expectations, and particularly those of entrepreneurs become more and more correct. What are these conditions, and what is the nature of the *process*? The assumptions of the perfect market do not provide answers to these questions. They assume them away.

There is the further question of 'how much knowledge' and 'what sort of knowledge' the different individuals must possess. The problem of the 'division of knowledge' is 'as important' as that of division of labour. Observation shows that prices tend to move towards cost due to individuals operating in the market place with different levels of knowledge, but non-Austrians often assume perfect knowledge and so evade the question.

Knowledge includes how goods can be obtained and used, and under what conditions they are so obtained and used. That is, it embraces the general question of reconciliation of objective and subjective data. Equilibrium assumes this reconciliation exists.

Facts can be learned by accident, or as a consequence of attempting to carry out a plan and discovering that facts differ from expectations. To proceed according to plan, knowledge is only required which relates to points which will be confirmed or corrected as the plan is executed. The relevant knowledge for equilibrium to hold is merely that which one is bound to hold given one's position; it is not all the knowledge which, if acquired accidentally, might be useful and lead to a change in plan. Thus this sort of equilibrium is not necessarily an optimum. Further conditions would be required, eg that each alternative use of each resource is known to at least some owner of that resource, and so all varying uses are interconnected.

As we shall discover, however, (in Chapter 5 below) even this stance is not fully representative of modern Austrianism. The stock of knowledge can never be fully exhausted (or exploited) as long as the economic resource of entrepreneurship and the human probability of error exist. For the moment, we consider the elements of entrepreneurship, the exchange process itself and how it can help bring about, if not an equilibrium, or even *the* equilibrium, certainly a movement towards it.

CATALLACTICS

Ever since Adam Smith wrote about the 'invisible hand' and the propensity of men to 'truck, barter and exchange' (Chapter 2, p10 above) trade has been one of the central topics of economic analysis.

Trade and exchange, in the sense Smith studied them, were spontaneous, unplanned activities guided only by the 'invisible hand' of self-interest. In his book, *Human Action*, von Mises defined this study of the exchange process as 'catallactics'.

Catallactics is derived from the Greek *katallatein* meaning 'to exchange', 'to make an enemy into a friend'. The word is a good one since no voluntary trade will be entered into unless *both* parties feel that they will be better off as a consequence. A catallaxy is the spontaneously produced market order where these exchanges take place. It arises because of the working of the 'invisible hand'. By definition, such a market does not have its objectives known in advance, and it cannot therefore be organised in a pre-designed manner from above.

Unlike a centrally planned society (or Robinson Crusoe on his island) production and consumption decisions are not predetermined. Nor can Lord Robbins' logic of choice be applied. The optimal allocation of known scarce resources to serve prescribed purposes implies knowledge and agreement in advance. The 'invisible hand', the 'catallaxy', works by competition. Competition between entrepreneurs is the mechanism used for discovering desired purposes that are not foreknown.

Before examining entrepreneurial competition, the way in which trade can 'make an enemy into a friend' will be examined. How is trade a beneficial activity?

One way to explain this is to use the well-known tool of indifference curve analysis. Indifference curves rest on three main assumptions:

(a) everyone wants more of many goods;

(b) there is always some amount of any good which will induce each person to give up some of any other good;

(c) each person's marginal evaluation of a good will decline the more he has of it.

The first assumption rests on the plausible belief that no one has enough of everything. And to get more of any particular good something else must be given up to obtain it. Few goods are 'free'. Even clean air can only be obtained by either incurring the costs of living and working in a rural area, or incurring commuting costs, or by all city dwellers forgoing in-city transport.

The second assumption follows the first. Provided a person can get sufficient in exchange of a particular good or goods, he will always be prepared to forgo some part of what he already has. The concept of the

43

marginal rate of substitution (MRS) rests on this assumption. The MRS of good X for good Y is the maximum amount of Y a person will give up to get one extra unit of X. It shows how much value the person places on one unit of X, at the margin, in terms of Y. The MRS is a purely subjective phenomenon. It shows his willingness to pay and is unique to him. It has nothing whatever to do with measures such as the costs of production. It depends solely on individual preference, and shows the strength of individual *wants*. It has nothing to do with what people say they *need*. Need is an irrelevant concept in the analysis of exchange. Wants, on the other hand, are basic to catallactics. They show how much a person is prepared to sacrifice in order to obtain what he wants.

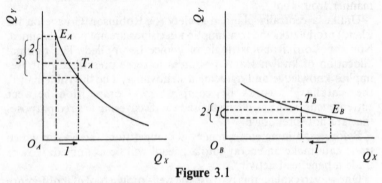

Figure 3.1

The third assumption asserts that what a person is prepared to give to get an extra unit of a good will decline the more of that good he has. The maximum price, the reservation price an individual will pay for a good will fall the more he has of it.

From these assumptions hypothetical indifference curves can be drawn.

Consider two individuals, *A* and *B*, in a two-good, *Y* and *X*, world, with indifference curves as shown in *Fig.* 3.1 With this framework it can now be shown that voluntarily negotiated trades are beneficial to both parties to an exchange. Exchange does not benefit one party at the expense of another. Each currently possesses bundles of *Y* and *X* as indicated by the marginal endowment points E_A and E_B. Their marginal evaluations of *Y* and *X* are not the same. *A* values *1X* at *3Ys* (or *1Y* at *1/3X*) but *B* thinks *1X* is only worth *1Y* (*1Y* is only worth *1X*).

Both individuals can be made better off if each acquires some of the good he values more highly from the other. For example, if *B* gives *1X* to *A* in exchange for *2Ys*, *B* moves to T_B and *A* to T_A (where T_A and T_B represent transaction or trade points).

B would have been willing to accept anything over *1Y* (to induce him to give up an *X*) and he receives *2Ys*. *A* would have been willing to pay anything under *3Ys* (to obtain an *X*) and he pays *2Ys*. Fig. 3.1 does not explicitly imply that points T_B and T_A will be the trades actually negotiated. It does not definitely state what exchange prices will be agreed upon, but the trades will take place in the direction of the arrows, and the price will be somewhere between *1Y* and *3Ys* for the traded *X*. Any price (in terms of *Y*) between these limits will result in both *A* and *B* becoming better off (moving to a higher isoquant). As they trade, their marginal evaluations come closer to each other. *A*'s MRS declines from 3:1 of *X* for *Y* and *B*'s MRS rises from its original 1:1 ratio. Trading continues until no further mutual gains are possible, that is until their respective MRSs are equal (at 2:1 in this instance).

An alternative geometric device, the Edgeworth Box, can be used to illustrate the same exchange procedure. In *Fig.* 3.2 the indifference curves for *A* and *B* have been superimposed after first swivelling *B*'s by 180°. The precise positions of the respective origins O_A and O_B are

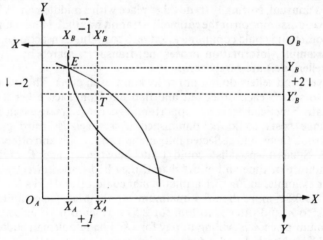

Figure 3.2

45

determined by ensuring that the original endowment points E_A and E_B coincide at E. In this way the total height of the Edgeworth Box measures the quantity of Ys held in aggregate by A and B, and similarly the breadth is restricted to the limited total of Xs held by the two individuals.

At E, since the indifference curves intersect, their slopes and hence their MRSs and the marginal valuations of X and Y held at A and B differ. The arrows indicate the trading process. When A moves from Y_A to Y_A' and gives up two units of Y, B acquires a corresponding amount. Similarly, A's positive acquisition of $1X$ from B is exactly counterbalanced by B's movement from X_B to X_B'. T will be a point of mutually beneficial trading and is equivalent to T_A and T_B in *Fig.* 3.2. No more trading will occur since, at this point, both A and B have identical valuations of Y in terms of X. Their respective indifference curves passing through T will be tangential to each other. A's minimum selling price for Y is the same as B's maximum buying price for Y (in terms of X).

Entrepreneurs can be regarded as middlemen—albeit very special types of middlemen. Here we will try to conceptualise the entrepreneurial function by looking first at the simplest type of middleman—the middleman who facilitates trading between A and B in the situations detailed in *Figs.* 3.1 and 3.2.

In the illustration described above, A and B traded face to face. This is unusual. Normally trade takes place with a middleman. Why? The basic assumption of the earlier illustration was that A and B knew each other and could communicate at zero cost. But transaction costs (for example, information processing, transport, search by buyer and seller, etc.) are rarely zero.

Buyers and sellers do not normally know each other. They would have to search each other out and find out from each other what mutually beneficial exchange opportunities existed. These search and exchange costs could be diminished if a specialist third party undertook them, and collected information about bids and offers for a fee. Such a specialist could trade between A and B at less expenditure of time and effort than if they had traded directly.

For example, in *Fig.* 3.1 a middleman could offer B $1.5Y$s for $1X$, which is $0.5Y$ more than B's minimum supply price. He could take that X to A and offer it to him for $2.5Y$s which is $0.5Y$ below the maximum price A is willing to pay for $1X$. The middleman ends up with $1Y$ and both A and B are better off than they were (they are on higher isoquants). Without the middleman, and with heavy trans-action costs (search, transport, bargaining), either the trade would not have taken place or exchange and transaction costs in excess of $1Y$ might have been incurred.

In *Fig.* 3.3 had the initial endowment point been such that the difference between the MRSs was $0.5Y$ and, had the cost of engaging in trade, even using a low cost specialist middleman, been $1Y$, then trade would not occur. A and B would remain at that endowment point and not move onto line $GCDF$.

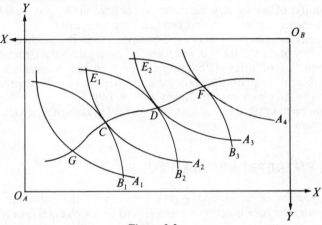

Figure 3.3

When a middleman spots the possibility to promote a trade between parties who have either previously been unaware that such a possibility exists, or who have been deterred by high transaction costs, then that middleman has spotted an entrepreneurial op-portunity. When he promotes that trade he is acting entrepreneurially. When his transaction costs, including any reward for the bearing of risk and any (actual or imputed) interest he must pay to the providers of capital, have been deducted from his income the residual is entrepreneurial profit.

In the conventional theory of price the objective is to define the conditions of optimisation in a given situation. For example, in terms of *Figs.* 3.1 and 3.2 given endowments E_A and E_B, given the tastes and preferences exemplified by the relevant isoquants for A and B, only

47

definite and precise values of the quantity variables X and Y, and of the price variables (the MRSs), are consistent with an equilibrium situation. The objective of conventional theory is to determine a point on the contract curve; it is not to tell us how that point is arrived at. In a search for equality of the marginal rates of substitution we are deflected from the more interesting and relevant tasks of asking why the entrepreneur/middleman arranges the mutually beneficial exchanges; of asking how he is made aware of opportunities for arranging trades; of asking how he informs A and B that trade possibilities exist; of asking how his function can be carried out more efficiently; of asking how he reacts to changes in the given data of endowments, preferences and production possibilities?

In conventional price theory 'efficiency' obtains in equilibrium. In the theory of competition as a process, efficiency does not depend on the equality of price with marginal cost or the equivalence of marginal rates of substitution, 'rather, it depends on the degree of success with which market forces can be relied upon to generate spontaneous corrections . . . at times of disequilibrium.' (Kirzner, 1974, pp6–7).

THE ENTREPRENEURIAL ROLE

This process of correction is the function of the entrepreneur. 'Entrepreneur means acting man in regard to the changes occurring in the market.' And when Mises (1963, p254) refers to the entrepreneur in this way he is not referring to capitalist or worker, to manager or employee, to producer or consumer. Any of these can be entrepreneur. 'Economics, in speaking of entrepreneurs, has in view not men, but a definite function' (Mises, 1966, pp246–50). So by inference any producer, consumer or resource owner who acts in response to change is, to a greater or lesser degree, an entrepreneur.

In equilibrium, therefore, there is no place for the function of entrepreneurship. In equilibrium, or what Mises called an 'evenly rotating economy' (Mises, 1966, pp246–50) there are no changes in the given data of endowments, technologies or preferences. In such an imaginary economy in which all transactions and physical conditions are repeated without change in each cycle of time there is no uncertainty. Everything is imagined to continue exactly as before, including all human ideas and goals. Under such fictitious constant repetitive conditions there can be no net change in any supply or demand and therefore there cannot be any changes in prices (or marginal valuations or marginal contributions). But as soon as these rigid assumptions of given data are abandoned it is clear that action must be affected by every data change. Since action is directed towards influencing the future, even if 'the future' is simply the next instant, then action is affected by every incorrectly anticipated data change between the initiation of the act and the period towards which the act is directed. 'Thus the outcome of action is always uncertain. Action is always speculation.' (Mises, 1963, p252 and p29 above).

This explains how every economic actor is an entrepreneur. There is no such thing as a perfectly predictable action. Moreover, this discussion can help highlight the differences and similarities between the Schumpeterian and Misesian concepts of 'entrepreneurship'.

In a chapter headed 'How the economic system generates evolution' Schumpeter (1939) identified innovation as one of the principal promoters of economic change and growth. Innovation was defined by Schumpeter to include not only the introduction of new products and techniques but also the opening up of new markets and supply sources, the improvement of management techniques and new distribution methods. The person responsible for doing these and other 'different things' is the entrepreneur or innovator. The entrepreneur, to Schumpeter, is a factor input and like other factor inputs must be rewarded. It is the payment for entrepreneurial services which forms Schumpeter's well-known concept of profit as a reward for innovation. 'It is the premium put upon a successful innovation in a capitalist society and is temporary by nature; it will vanish in the subsequent process of competition and adaptation.' (Schumpeter, 1948, p83).

Here are highlighted both the differences and the similarities between the Misesian and Schumpeterian entrepreneur. Mises' entrepreneur, like Schumpeter's, acts for anticipated personal gain. But the Misesian entrepreneur is *any* human actor motivated by gain. In *Figs*. 3.1 and 3.2 two individuals, *A* and *B*, gained from the process of trade. In discussion it was shown that the trade could also have been initiated by a middleman. The spotting of the opportunity for gain, the initiation of the necessary action, and the capturing of the (uncertain) profit are all the functions of an entrepreneur. At some stage of the exchange *each* of *A*, *B* and the middleman had to act entrepreneurially. It is possible that each incurred similar entrepreneurial effort and reaped similar rewards, but it is more probable that one of the three assumed the greatest part (but not the whole) of the entrepreneurial role. No one can be wholly passive, no one can take totally predictable actions, no one can opt out of entrepreneurship except in equilibrium.

So both Schumpeter's and Mises' entrepreneurs act in accordance with the 'invisible hand' in order to obtain profit or gain. In this way their notions can be reconciled. But the differences are more important than the similarities. Schumpeter's entrepreneur moves the economy away from one equilibrium towards another higher level equilibrium. Mises' entrepreneur, however, helps move the economy towards equilibrium, but that equilibrium is itself an ever changing and unattainable objective. Schumpeter's entrepreneur can be studied within the context of an evenly rotating economy where particular individual changes are initiated by the innovator and the logical effects of these particular changes deduced via the principles of marginal equivalency. This can be a valid and useful method of analysis but it tells us little of the market process itself.

The concept of the entrepreneur can now be seen to be much fuller and richer than it appears at first sight. The entrepreneur (be he producer, consumer, middleman or resource owner) does far more than merely bring together two parties and facilitate a mutually beneficial exchange between them (as in *Figs.* 3.1 and 3.2). The entrepreneur is the person who is *alert* to the presence of such opportunities before anyone else perceives them.

The entrepreneur notes, *ex ante*, that the indifference curves of consumers are different tomorrow from what they are today. He notes *ex ante*, that the production isoquants of producers are not the same tomorrow as they are today.

The entrepreneur may make mistakes in his predictions, or he may be correct: in which case he makes losses or profits. The entrepreneur must choose which prediction he believes to be correct. But he cannot simply choose to facilitate a process which equates *current* marginal valuations. Professor Shackle says:

Decision is choice amongst rival available courses of action. We can choose only what is still unactualised; we can choose only amongst imaginations and figments. Imagined actions . . . can have only imagined consequences. (Shackle, 1970, p106).

Even without changes in basic market data (consumer tastes, production possibilities and resource endowments) decisions made today generate a new series of decisions tomorrow. Today's decisions (the commencement of the market process) are made in ignorance of these basic market data. As the market process unfolds this ignorance is reduced and each market participant revises his bid and offer prices in the light of what has occurred and what he has now learnt about others to or from whom he may wish to sell or buy. *The process is inherently competitive* since each successive set of offers and bids is more attractive than the preceding one. That is, every individual offer or bid is being made with the awareness that all others are now being made with fuller knowledge of the advantageous opportunities available. Since that is so, each individual participant knows that he cannot offer less attractive trading opportunities than his competitors. He (and they) must continually inch ahead of his (their) rivals.

THE COMPETITIVE PROCESS

Even without changes in basic market data this competitive movement towards equilibrium brought about by entrepreneurs must occur. If it did not, the potential traders would not trade. In terms of *Figs*. 3.1, 3.2 and 3.3 *A* and *B* would go to market and return home empty handed. Would-be traders (would-be self-improvers motivated by the invisible hand) would fail to realise that they could exchange unless they (or a middleman) *learn to alter* their bid and offer prices, that is unless someone acts in an entrepreneurial manner. The competitive process is 'analytically inseparable' from entrepreneurship. (Kirzner, 1974, p16).

Now let us examine changes in the basic market data. If technology and/or tastes change, or if new types of quantities of resources are discovered, then any of the information contained in *Fig*. 3.2 relating to the indifference curves of either *A* and/or *B* and/or to the dimensions of the Edgeworth Box itself, and so to the relative position of the endowment point *E*, will be affected. Market disequilibrium is not then simply a pattern of prices and quantities subject to change under competitive pressure from the entrepreneurial arbitrage function. It is not then simply a case of an actual or hypothetical middleman offering a seller a marginally higher price and a buyer a marginally lower price than would satisfy either, and pocketing the (net of costs) difference as profit. With changes in the basic data this same process is occurring as the 'middleman' offers buyers other marginal improvements (such as a wider product range, or a higher quality product) and/or as he provides sellers with conditions or opportunities for sale not previously on offer.

To accomplish these things the 'middleman' or entrepreneur must generally also incur costs. But his net-of-costs profit does not arise through *him* exchanging something *he* values for something *he* values more. It comes about rather because he has been alert enough to discover sellers and buyers with such different valuations. Pure entrepreneurial profit arises from '*the discovery of something obtainable for nothing at all*'. (Emphasis by Kirzner, 1974, p144, in original.)

Conceptually then, entrepreneurial profit is the reward which accrues to that unique someone who is alert enough to take it. The very act of grasping what is already there will alert less wakeful entrepreneurs to do the same so that over time the combination of arbitrage and entry ensures that such profits fall to zero. Such a process will work itself out competitively or begin again when another such opportunity appears and is noticed by the most alert to have emerged.

Of course, the entrepreneur in practice may well have to involve other market participants before he can grasp his profits. He may, but need not, combine the entrepreneurial role with that of one of these other participants. Other market actors include consumers, producers and resource-owners.

An entrepreneurial consumer, as an individual, may seek out improved exchange opportunities. So too might a producer. But it is worth pointing out that both production and consumption can be subsumed under exchange. For example, Robert Clower (1977) argues:

An ongoing exchange economy with specialist traders *is* a production economy since there is no bar to any merchant capitalist acquiring labour services and other resources as a 'buyer' and transforming them (repackaging, reprocessing into new forms, etc) into outputs that are unlike the original inputs and are 'sold' accordingly as are commodities that undergo no such transformation. In short, a production unit *is* a particular type of middleman or trading specialist.

Austrians such as Mises, Hayek and Kirzner would agree with much of Clower's view. But they would disagree with Clower when he says 'that "capitalists" are just individuals who have the wit and forethought to exploit profit opportunities by . . . engaging in the "production" of both trading services and new types of commodities.' Those with the 'forethought' are the entrepreneurs. Capitalists are resource owners who *may* combine that function with that of entrepreneurship.

One needs to look no further than the nineteenth century history of retail co-operatives in the United Kingdom to see how consumers, too, can perceive entrepreneurial opportunities and exploit them. The fact that the retail co-operatives came to employ resources of land and labour and have accumulated trading capital to purchase other forms of stocks and equipment may mean that some entrepreneurial acts in the modern, consumer co-operative are inspired by resource owners such as managers or capitalists but the proximate entrepreneurship was undoubtedly that of consumers.

At the individual level also, consumers seek out favourable exchange opportunities. But in the modern industrial economy the costs of entrepreneurial activity, the costs of generating alertness to the potential of gain, is more generally carried out by resource owners, producers and consumers of intermediate products rather than by consumers of final products. It tends to be *firms* which carry out competitive price adjustments in both a situation of static and of changing market data. Final consumers tend to buy or not to buy according to the valuations they place or will place on the offered commodities[1]. The more complex the economy, the greater the variety of goods and services available, the more likely this is to be true. The consumer has only a limited time span in which to carry out entrepreneurial search (there are a fixed number of hours in the day). Yet the range of purchase opportunities continues always to increase. It is not surprising, then, that more and more of the entrepreneurial role is being undertaken by producers.

Not only is the firm (or the entrepreneurial component of the firm) constantly adjusting or being forced to adjust its offered price to bring it closer into line with consumer wants, the firm is also constantly attempting to adjust its whole commodity offering. In the light of changing technologies, resources and consumer tastes, the entrepreneurial component in the firm will not only be attempting to bring bid and offer prices marginally closer together[2] but will also be attempting to bring the range and quality of apparently and potentially tradeable goods and services closer together.

In this way product differentiation, research and development, selling cost and advertising will all be engaged in by competitive firms attempting better to satisfy consumer demand.

When a producer-entrepreneur incurs costs to satisfy what he perceives *will be* consumer demand, he is doing so to win anticipated revenue in excess of his anticipated costs. He will gain that anticipated profit only if he competes more successfully than others in meeting demand. His costs will include the normally defined manufacturing costs and also the conventionally defined advertising costs. But no 'single penny of the outlay . . . (manufacturing or advertising costs) . . . can be perceived as anything but costs incurred in order to "sell"'. (Kirzner, 1974, p144).

In Chapter 5 more recent developments in Austrian micro-economics will be tackled. We will examine the entrepreneur's role in more detail. The importance of information, uncertainty and transaction costs will be discussed more explicitly. And the part which planning has to play, already discussed in this chapter, will be expanded upon. First, however, in Chapter 4 we turn from micro to Austrianism's response to macroeconomics.

NOTES

1. Final consumers are entrepreneurs in that they search for better trade possibilities. But, in general, more effort is incurred by firms placing before consumers an array of such opportunities from which to choose. Firms search out consumers more actively than consumers search out firms
2. Only marginally, in order to capture as much business as possible from higher priced rivals; not totally, otherwise the entrepreneurial profit arising from different marginal valuations will not exist

REFERENCES

K J Arrow, 'Towards a Theory of Price Adjustment,' (1959) in Y Brosen (ed), *The Competitive Economy*, (1975), General Learning Press.
R Clower, Private communication to Joan Robinson cited in 'What are the Questions?' *Journal of Economic Literature*, (1977).

J B Egger, 'The Austrian Method' (1978) in L M Spadaro (ed), *New Directions in Austrian Economics*, Sheed, Andrews and McMeel.

M Friedman, *Essays in Positive Economics*, University of Chicago Press, (1974).

F A Hayek, 'Economics and knowledge', *Economica*, (1937); 'The use of knowledge in society', *American Economic Review*, (1945).

J R Hicks and W Weber (eds), *Carl Menger and the Austrian School of Economics*, Oxford University Press, (1973).

J Kirkpatrick, 'Theory and History in Marketing' *Managerial and Decision Economics*, 1983.

I Kirzner, 'Divergent Approaches in Libertarian Economic Thought', *Intercollegiate Review*, (1967); *Competition and Entrepreneurship*, University of Chicago Press, (1974); 'On the Method of Austrian Economics' in E G Dolan (ed), *The Foundations of Modern Austrian Economics*, Sheed and Ward, (1976).

K Menger, 'Austrianism, Marginalism and Mathematical Economics' in L von Mises, *Human Action*, Henry Regnery, (1963 edition); *Human Action*, Henry Regnery, (1966); *The Ultimate Foundations of Economic Science,* Sheed, Andrews and McMeel, (1976).

P J McNulty, 'Economic theory and the meaning of competition', *Quarterly Journal of Economics* (1968).

M Rizzo, 'Praxeology and Econometrics: A Critique of Positivist Economics' in Spadaro, op. cit., (1978).

L Robbins, *The Nature and Significance of Economic Science*, Macmillan, (1935); Economics and Political Economy', *American Economic Review*, (1981).

M Rothbard, 'Praxeology: The Methodology of Modern Austrian Economics', in E G Dolan *op. cit.*, (1976).

J A Schumpeter, *Business Cycles*, Harrap (1939); *Capitalism, Socialism and Democracy*, Harrap, (1948).

G L S Shackle, *Expectation, Enterprise and Profit*, George Allen and Unwin, (1970).

B Summers, 'The division of knowledge', *The Freeman,* (1977).

4 The Austrian Macro Retort

Given the stress laid by Austrians on subjectivism and methodological individualism it would seem that a macro position would be definitionally proscribed. However, this is too simplistic a view. Austrians would certainly agree that what is happening in the macroeconomy can only be understood by studying its micro-foundations. This is not the same as ignoring the macro situation, rather it is a method of approach which explores the problem from the ground up and does not discount the interactions of component markets of the whole as being at best a separate subject of study and at worst as irrelevant.

In the following pages we deal first with some problems and fallacies of economic aggregation. Secondly we examine the Austrian view of capital and interest. Thirdly money, and its role in the business cycle is studied. The way in which Austrians and Quantity Theorists differ on these issues is expanded. Finally, more recent attempts to make these differences clear to those trained in the non-Austrian tradition are summarised.

DANGERS OF ECONOMIC AGGREGATION

In the previous chapter the importance of information for economics was stressed. 'When we use numbers we lose information' (Pirie, 1982, p9). In a nutshell this is the case against aggregative macroeconomics as traditionally studied. When one numerically controlled machine tool or one consumer is under discussion numbers are irrelevant. But numbers become useful immediately two consumers or two machine tools are considered. This concept of 'two' implicitly suggests similarities or even identities which in all probability do not exist. No two apples are the same. But immediately the study of one apple, its weight, shape, taste and so on is given up for the study of the average weight and shape of two apples some information is foregone. Even more information is lost when the discussion moves to the level of three fruit (one of which is a pear), or four foods (one of which is a fish), or five goods (one of which is a table). And this is precisely what macroeconomics does when it reduces the total number of markets in the economy to four: labour, goods, bonds and money. The fallacy of adding an airline pilot and a surgeon to conceptually arrive at two homogeneous workers; of adding an apple and a machine tool to obtain two goods; a General Motors share certificate with one for a hat store to obtain two bonds; and a monetary note to a bank account to arrive at two monetary units is apparently obvious. Information is forfeited by the aggregation process.

Yet the *minimising* of information disparities is one of the chief outcomes of economic activity. Price differentials in individual markets signal to entrepreneurs that information is imperfect and asymmetric and so they act so as to encourage exchange and thus *increase* the information available to market participants (p35 above). Macroeconomic activity, on the other hand, uses numerical data with minimal information content and bases policy decisions designed for the management of the macroeconomy upon it. For Austrians this is both fallacious and dangerous.

For example, common goals of macroeconomic policy are to stabilise the price level, encourage full employment by use of the Keynesian multiplier and to control the money supply.

To take these in order of mention. Austrians would seriously question whether there is such a thing as 'the' price level. Hayek (1978, p15) has argued that the *ex post* statistical construct of a price index is not representative of reality in the sense that observations in the physical sciences would be such a representation. In 1955 he wrote (p3) that 'what we regard as the field of physics may well be the . . . phenomena where the number of significantly connected variables of different kinds is sufficiently small . . . to study them as if they formed a closed system for which we can observe and control all the determining factors'. This is certainly not the case with index numbers which attempt to measure changes in 'the' price level.

There, attempts are often made to contrast a monetary unit with 'the' basket of goods bought for the provisioning of 'the' household. As the amount of money required to buy this basket changes so the purchasing power of money and the general price level has changed. But as Mises (1966, pp200–2) points out neither the hypothetical housewife nor her imaginary basket are 'constant elements'. The qualities of the goods in the basket change. New goods appear and old ones cease to be bought. Consumer valuations change which in turn alters both demand and production. In consequence individual prices rise or fall changing the 'mix' of the basket as consumers buy more of the latter and less of the former. It is also necessary to attach weights to the basket's contents. The choice of weighting in turn will vary the basket's price. Even so the previous point, of changing relative prices and so quantities, will render any weighting system continuously obsolete. And none of this takes into account the statistical problems involved in obtaining the base for the original 'average housewife' and 'average basket' nor the fact that no such basket will ever contain all available consumer choice options in any case. In the real world of choosing human beings, whose actions are both purposive and individually unique, no index number, however sophisticated its statistical construction, can indicate accurately what is happening to the general price level or the purchasing power of money. It then follows, as night does day, that macroeconomic attempts to maintain the stability of 'the' price level must be in vain.

The Keynesian multiplier is another example of the dangers of fallacious aggregation. Here we will deal not with the multiplier concept *per se* and the notion that national income may expand by more than the net 'addition to the value of the capital' stock (Keynes, 1960, p62). Rather we take Lachmann's point (1976, p157) that if 'the stock is unmeasurable how can we tell what is an addition to it?' With these two unknowns, if unknown they are, then fiscal and monetary stimuli to the economy for multiplier reasons become at best non-operational and at worst counter-productive.

That capital does indeed defy aggregation is easy to show. The primary reason is not that capital goods are themselves diverse in their physical characteristics. A common measuring rod such as money could overcome some such difficulties (although then both the information loss and index number problems would arise, particularly when considering additions to the stock after the original valuation date).

Hicks identified two ways in which a monetary rather than a 'materialist' yardstick could be used to measure the capital stock. In 1963 (pp342–8) he argued that it might gauged by the 'consumption goods that are foregone to get it'. (Nonetheless these sacrifices themselves would have been heterogeneous in kind and in time.) For most decisions, however, bygones are bygones and in 1974 Hicks specified the more widely accepted notion that the stock of capital goods be measured by aggregating the expected contributions of each to future streams of output.

Austrians reject the view that the three alternatives are mutually exclusive, but also argue that no method or methods of capital measurement is adequate. To ignore the heterogeneous characteristics of the capital stock is to deny the presence or absence of complementarity of specific capital goods. The issue of whether the productive purpose of one particular good is dependent not only on the plans of its owner but also on the plans of other producers is sidestepped. But as Lachmann (1976b, p146) points out: 'In the absence of perfect foresight on the part of capital owners, some malinvestment is inevitable, and some of the capital accumulated vanishes from the scene'. This 'perfect foresight' is not and can never be present either in conditions of a physical inventory of capital, a monetary evaluation of whatever kind, or of both simultaneously.

Kirzner (1976, p139) highlights the futility of both financial and physical measures. 'A man's future plans depend not only on the aggregate size of his capital stock but also very crucially upon the particular properties of the various goods making up that stock.' But only in an evenly rotating economy is perfect foresight present. Kirzner goes on (p140):

[decisions] must be made as to how a resource is to be deployed before one can talk about its future contribution to output. Because there are alternative uses . . . and alternative clusters of complementary inputs . . . it is confusing to see a resource as representing a definite future output flow before the necessary decisions . . . have been made.

And, one could add, before the presumed consumer responses have occurred or have not occurred, as the case may be.

As Lachman (1976a, p153) points out it is only in equilibrium that 'capital *can* be measured, . . . only here [is] the discounted present value of the highest income stream obtainable from a given capital resource . . . exactly equal to its cost of reproduction . . . otherwise there would be investment or disinvestment, neither of which is compatible with a stationary state . . . [otherwise] . . . replacement cost and [this] . . . discounted future income stream will diverge . . .

[the] real reason for our inability to measure capital lies in the subjective nature of expectations concerning future income streams.'

Here Lachmann echoes Keynes (p23 above). The point that capital measurement is impossible because of aggregation and associated difficulties has now been made. The danger of using the Keynesian multiplier while unavoidably basing it on misinformation is obvious. However, the purpose of Austrian economics as it is now developing should not be viewed as simply negative and iconoclastic. As we pointed out earlier (p51) the study of the competitive market process is an attempt to ascertain how and why unnoticed opportunities are discovered. There is no reason to think that economists will always be unable to understand the way in which expectations are formed and how tastes change. That may bring us no nearer to solving the problem of capital measurement but it may help suggest the type of environment which will foster economic growth. And it is this latter goal, after all, which the Keynesian multiplier was intended to deal with.

Finally, in this section on the hazards of aggregation we briefly look at the concept of the money supply. Money is frequently believed to be closely associated with inflation or depression (pp18–9 and the attempts by many governments to control inflation in the 1970s and 1980s by managing the money supply). The issue here is not the validity of such a view but rather to discover what is meant by 'money'. Any current economics text provides an almost bewildering array of differently defined monetary aggregates each of which has at some time received support from some writer as measuring 'the' supply of money (for example M_1 M_2 M_3, the monetary base, and even money GDP itself). Mises (1971, Chapter 1) defines money by isolating its 'primary' purpose which is that of a medium of exchange. It is what all other goods are traded for and it is the mode of final payment for all such goods. As such it includes not only the stock of 'standard cash' (whether gold, warehouse receipts for gold or real or fiat coins) but also whatever is subjectively believed or perceived to be the operational equivalent of standard cash. Thus as Rothbard (1978, pp144–6) points out any deposits repayable on demand are part of the money supply. And this is the case even when a fractional reserve banking system is in operation because although such deposits cannot, *in fact*, be repaid on demand (at least not simultaneously) market operators *believe* that they can. And, of course, it is with the perceptions of market participants and the impact of these perceptions on market behaviour, that Austrian economics is primarily concerned. As long as market participants believe this then demand deposits are regarded by Austrians as part of the money supply.

As Rothbard points out (1978, p144) when Mises wrote his *Theory of Money and Credit* in 1912 and argued for the inclusion of demand deposits in the money supply he was ahead of most contemporary writers. Irving Fisher in *The Purchasing Power of Money*, published in 1913 still felt it necessary to distinguish between standard cash and demand deposits (a distinction no economist of any school would make today). Mises, however, in 1912 (1971, p68) argued that any deposit of cash which could be redeemed on demand was simply a *claim* transaction where the cash was exchanged for a real or pseudo warehouse receipt. On the other hand, where money is deposited and can only be redeemed at some future date a *credit* transaction has taken place. A 'present good' has been exchanged against a 'future good'. It might appear then that what is money is any liquid asset. Mises (1971, p286) wrote in 1912 that this 'is the cause of much obscurity'. The acid test, however, is not liquidity, since all assets can be sold on markets, but whether the asset is redeemable at a fixed rate, at par, in money' (Rothbard, 1978, p149). There should be no friction. Money is not under discussion if it is 'necessary in each individual case for the parties to the transaction to begin by coming to a special agreement as to the present price to be paid for the claim that would not fall due until some future time' (Mises, 1971, p286). Thus bills, bonds, stocks, shares, bread, automobiles, and so on are excluded from the Austrian definition of money.

Rothbard (1978, pp149–50) argues also that *cash surrender values* of life insurance policies should be included as money, as should time deposits and shares in building societies or savings and loan associations since *de facto* all are redeemable on demand for known amounts even if a *de jure* waiting period can be imposed. Again people act on the *de facto* situation. Certainly this view is consistent with Mises' and has not been challenged by other Austrian writers.

It is interesting to note the apparent unanimity of Austrians on aggregation as a means of measuring the money supply. Probably this is because, in this case, one of the stumbling blocks of aggregation, namely heterogeneity of the component parts, has been effectively removed by careful definition.

CAPITAL AND INTEREST

Few topics in economic thought have generated more heat than those of capital and interest. One reason for this is that interest is regarded by many as in some sense being 'unearned' and thus unethical. As a corollary it would be held that produced goods belong to labour in their entirety and not to the providers of capital who receive the interest. We have already seen that Adam Smith made obeisance to the labour theory of value (p9 above) and hence it is no surprise to discover that the classical economists as a whole also tended to follow this belief. Böhm-Bawerk (1975, p2) in reviewing the labour theory of value summarises the way it leads to the view that interest is exploitative as follows: 'Interest . . . consists in a portion of the product of the labour of others, acquired by exploiting the situation which places the worker under coercion.' All goods are the product of labour. Yet the worker does not receive the full value of his efforts. Private property provides the capitalist with control over the capital goods without which the labourer cannot produce. The wage negotiated enables the capitalist to retain part of the value of the workers' output. Since the worker desires to obtain the necessities of life this forces him to accept a wage lower than the value of his product. The capitalist receives the difference (interest) at no cost to himself.

Böhm-Bawerk tackles the problem of capital and interest by examining the claims of two of the major writers in the area: Karl Rodbertus and Karl Marx. (Rodbertus he argues, is the 'best presenter' of the exploitation theory of interest and Marx the most 'widely recognised' (Böhm-Bawerk, 1975, p13)).

Böhm-Bawerk's explanation of capital and interest had many facets. Here we will dwell on one in particular, since some of the others have been modified or discarded by later writers. Böhm-Bawerk's principle refutation of the exploitation theory of interest was his emphasis that subjective valuations differ in the presence of a time factor. The phenomenon of time preference was illustrated simply by Böhm-Bawerk (1975, p32) by what he called the 'crudest empirical test': '. . . if you ask 1000 persons to choose between a gift of $1000 today and $1000 50 years from today all 1000 of them will prefer to have it today.'

If people do value the same good today more highly than the same good tomorrow then the position of Rodbertus and Marx must be carefully scrutinised. In a situation where the only inputs are labour and freely available natural resources Böhm-Bawerk agrees that it is (p31):

completely just . . . that the worker . . . receive the entire value of his product [but this] can reasonably be interpreted to mean either that he is to receive the full *present* value of his product *now* or that he is to get the entire *future* value in the *future*. But . . . the socialists interpret it to mean that the worker is to receive the entire *future* value of his product *now*.

He continues (p39) 'that is not a *fulfilment but a violation* of the fundamental principle that the worker is entitled to receive as his wage the value of what he produces'. Böhm-Bawerk illustrates this by placing the argument in a purely socialist state and imagining it takes five years to build an engine, that five men work at it, each for one year. If the completed engine commands a price of $5500 should each man get $1100? The answer given is negative. The first worker should get more and the last least. (At a 5% simple interest rate the figures would be $1200, $1150, $1100, $1050 and $1000 for the five men respectively.)

The reason for the wage differential is interest. But why has interest arisen? Because of the universal phenomenon of time preference an earlier 'worker cannot or will not wait until his product has been fully completed' (p31). Certainly the 'worker will get justice if he gets all that he has laboured to produce up to this point' (Böhm-Bawerk, 1975, p31). But one physical fifth of an engine at the end of year one is not worth the same as one physical fifth of an engine at the end of year five (even if the physical characteristics of each fifth are identical). The former is worth less because of time preference. But the hypothetical wages Böhm-Bawerk awarded are, in fact, equal (as well as totalling to the whole value of the engine). $1000 paid to the first worker at the end of year one is equal (at 5% simple interest) to $1200 at the end of five years. Certainly the 5% is an arbitrary figure for illustration only. The actual rate of interest will depend on actual time preferences as revealed in the market place. That these exist, however, is not in dispute. The interest rate is 'a direct result of the fact that we humans live out our lives in a temporal world, that our today with its needs and cares comes before our tomorrow' (Böhm-Bawerk, 1975, p34).

Böhm-Bawerk's use of the time preference concept as a critique was equally valid in negating the works of both Rodbertus and Marx on the exploitation theory of interest (Böhm-Bawerk, 1975, p59). However, although Böhm-Bawerk was seen by Mises (1971, p339) as being the 'first to clear the way' to an understanding of present goods, future goods and interest he has been strongly criticised by other Austrian economists on his notion of capital. Thus Carl Menger is quoted as saying that his theory of capital was 'one of the greatest blunders ever committed' (cited in Schumpeter, 1954, p847). Kirzner (1979, p81) suggests that one major reason for this disagreement was Böhm-Bawerk's measurement of capital. He defined it as the aggregate of intermediate products, that is the totality of the produced means of production. We have already noted (p59) that Austrians discount the possibility of measuring the aggregate of an economy's capital stock, whether the yardstick be the goods themselves, or the common denominator of money. However, as early as 1922 in his book *Socialism* Mises (1981, p106) argued that not only should the concept of capital be clearly distinguished from that of capital goods but that it should be analysed and discussed at the micro level not the macro. That is, in economic practice firms and individuals measure capital monetarily for decision-making purposes having an eye to the future outcomes of these decisions. Consequently it is at that level and from that perspective that economists should examine capital. Mises (1966, pp260–4) argues that capital expresses in monetary terms the net wealth (assets minus liabilities: capital goods plus net savings) belonging to a firm or person operating in the market. It is only by use of such an accounting concept that the losses or profits (net additions to capital) of contemplated actions can be estimated and those of completed actions can be calculated.

Capital, therefore, depends on a market economy to provide the monetary values (i.e. prices) for the accountant and businessman to aggregate and compare. As Kirzner put it (1979, p78): it 'is properly defined as the subjectively perceived monetary value of the owner's equity . . .'. Actions are taken with capital in order to achieve (when successful) profits. 'To direct production towards profit simply means to direct it to satisfy other peoples demand' (Mises, 1981, p124).

But how are the monetary values of capital goods determined on the market? Böhm-Bawerk was certainly correct when he described capitalist production as a 'roundabout' method which requires more time but compensates for the delay by producing more and better end-products. It is these final goods and services which consumers actually want. Final goods and services are described by Menger as goods of a lower (or first) order. The capital goods which produce them are goods of a higher order (Menger, 1976, p150). Thus second order goods are capital or producers' goods only one stage in production removed from the final consumers' good. Third order goods are capital goods one further stage removed and so on.

Menger argues that:

requirements for goods of higher order is dependent upon the goods they serve to produce having . . . expected *value* . . . [W]e do not need [such] goods . . . for the production of goods of lower order that have no expected value . . . We therefore have the principle that the value of goods of higher order is dependent upon the expected value of the goods of lower order they serve to produce . . . [Thus] the value of goods of higher order cannot be the *determining* factor in the prospective value of the corresponding goods of lower order (emphases in original).

Note Menger's consistent use of the word 'expected'. It is not 'the current value . . . but rather the . . . prospective values of the goods of lower order' which is relevant. Thus again, as we saw in the previous chapter, the Austrian emphasis on *ex ante* entrepreneurial behaviour is critical and reinforces in turn Mises' argument that capital goods should be regarded as an accounting concept for forward looking decisions (which will, of course, sometimes be incorrect) at the micro, acting level, rather than a heterogeneous macro aggregation which because it embraces all micro values, right or wrong, will inevitably be incorrect.

This Mengerian view of the productive process enables Mises to tell us what originary interest is not. It is not 'the price paid for the services of capital' (Mises, 1966, p526), nor is it the 'income derived from the utilisation of capital goods' (p524), and so by extension *it cannot be an impetus to save nor a reward for abstaining from consumption* (p527). Without time preference the price of a factor input (land, labour or capital) would equal the 'undiscounted sum of the original values of the future services attached to it' (Kirzner, 1979, p86). But because time preference is universal factor prices reflect only the discounted value of their services and these values produce the Böhm-Bawerkian flow of interest.

This, originary interest, is the ratio of the 'valuation of present goods as against future goods' (Mises, 1966, p527). To take Böhm-

Bawerk's arithmetically trite and slightly misleading example: the engine builder who received $1050 at the end of year 4 got $50 more than the final worker one year later. This gives a ratio of 1050:1000 or 1.05 (= 5% as a percentage). Mises points out that it is not the loan market which determines this rate. The loan market simply reflects changing valuations of present to future goods. Moreover, the actual market interest rate also includes, as well as originary interest, an entrepreneurial profit component due to uncertainty of repayment and/or anticipated changes in the future value of the goods under consideration (Mises, p536). We will return to the Austrian view of interest in the final section of this chapter. Meantime we will also find the concept of value as we turn to examine the unique explanation Austrians provide for the existence of the trade cycle.

MONEY AND THE BUSINESS CYCLE

The founders of the Austrian School, Menger, Böhm-Bawerk and Wieser were never greatly concerned with the trade cycle. It was left to the next generation of Austrians to provide solutions to the problem. These came particularly from Mises' 1912 book on *Money and Credit* (1971), Hayek's 1931 *Prices and Production*, and work by Haberler (1932) and others. We will look first at the most recent writings of Hayek (i.e. post World War II) and then return to some of the work of the 1930s which shows how the Austrian view of the trade cycle bridged the gap between explanations which concentrated exclusively on only monetary or only on 'real' forces. In turn this enabled pre-war Austrians to reject 'real' solutions for Depressions (such as Keynes' (1931, p39) proposed electrification of Britain's railways) as being more harmful than helpful.

F A Hayek (1977, pp330–3) argued that inflation could only temporarily reduce unemployment. Like Friedman's view of the expectations-adjusted Phillips Curve, Hayek's explanation is also based on the fact that transactors only have imperfect information. The allocation of resources in an economy is a complex task. It is inevitable that mistakes will be made, whether the economy is controlled by the market or by a command mechanism, Either individual businessmen or the central planner could fail to perceive consumers' wants correctly. Information costs, however, are much lower in the exchange economy because individual entrepreneurs need only concern themselves with those data relevant to the particular markets in which they are operating. In a centrally planned economy, all information must be collected and collated and analysed simultaneously in one place. In either situation mistakes will be made.

For example, labour can be drawn into jobs where there is insufficient demand for the final product to pay wages. In a decentralised economy this normally becomes quickly apparent. Firms which overestimated the demand for their product will fail and the workers employed there will seek out better (consumer supported) jobs.

However, during unanticipated inflation, even firms making products for which there is insufficient demand will prosper. This is because employers are able to hire workers at a given wage rate which is low compared to the price of the final product when it is eventually sold. Indeed, both worker and employer are probably unaware that the wage rate agreed on is low in comparison with what the price of the final product will become.

If the demand for the final product, however, is such that in the absence of inflation the selling price is neither what the employer originally expected, *nor* a higher money figure, but is a figure lower than both of these, then the firm's expected profit is either less than anticipated or is a loss. The firm would then cut back on employment or even go out of business. With unanticipated inflation, however, the originally hoped for selling price, or more, can be obtained, and labour will continue to be employed. However, as soon as workers anticipate the inflation they will cease to be content to work for the original (and now relatively low) money wage. The temporary profits created by the inflation will vanish, and firms producing products for which there is insufficient actual demand will cut back on employment or go out of business.

Inflation (as in the Phillips curve analysis) can temporarily reduce unemployment by postponing the time when misdirected labour will be laid off. It is always ultimately necessary to fire workers where there is insufficient real demand for what their labour produces. The deficiency in demand may be because of a change in taste by consumers or errors in judgement by businessmen. In either case, inflation makes it more difficult to perceive the actual lack of demand and postpones the inevitable reallocation of resources which must occur.

This argument only holds, as stated, if the inflation is unanticipated. Transactors can adjust their behaviour to the market's real needs if the inflation is anticipated. As a corollary, only a continuously accelerating rate of inflation can indefinitely postpone the inevitable unemployment (the stagflation) which will emerge when the misdirected labour begins to look for jobs that can be supported by the actual pattern of demands.

This of course begs the question. Why? Although changes are continually taking place in the economy—some industries are growing, some declining—why should there ever be a *general* boom or slump? The only phenomenon which permeates the whole economy is money and it is to this we must look for an answer and explanation. Why should rises or falls in the demand for or supply of money generate the business cycle?

The main problem is why is there suddenly a '*cluster*' of business errors? Businessmen and entrepreneurs are market experts (otherwise they would not survive) and why should they all make mistakes simultaneously? A secondary issue is why do capital goods industries fluctuate more widely than consumer goods ones? And a third question is why does the quantity of money rise in a boom and fall in a slump?

The business cycle is generated by monetary expansion and contraction. (Here we follow the arguments of Mises, 1966, pp571–86). Assume the money supply is constant. People will have a *time preference*. The less consumption they prefer now, the lower will be their time preference, and the lower the 'pure interest rate'. The proportion of income devoted to saving and investment will be higher and the capital stock of the economy will be built up, lengthening the production process as the division of labour increases. Higher time preferences will have the reverse effect. The final market rate of interest will reflect the pure interest rate plus or minus the relevant entrepreneurial rewards and inflation rate.

When new money is printed it appears as if the supply of savings has increased. Interest rates fall and businessmen are misled into borrowing additional funds to finance extra investment activity. This investment occurs first in capital goods industries rather than consumer goods ones. The 'process of production' is lengthened. This would be of no consequence if it had been the outcome of a genuine fall in time preferences—it could be sustained indefinitely—but the change was government induced. The new money reaches factor owners in the form of wages, rent and interest. Given unchanged time preferences, the factor owners will then spend the higher money incomes in their existing consumption: investment proportions. That is, demand will move back from the higher orders to the lower orders of production (to industries closer to the final consumer). Capital goods industries will find their expansion has been in error and mal-investments have been incurred. Losses will be made due to entrepreneurial misjudgements and the mal-investments must some-how be liquidated. In short, 'booms' of this type are wasteful misinvestment due to government interference with the market place. The 'crisis' occurs when consumers attempt to re-establish their desired consumption–income proportions. The ensuing 'depression' follows as night follows day. It is simply the process of adjustment which the economy makes to correct the errors and the wastes of the boom. It continues until consumer demands are efficiently met once again.

This Hayekian and Misesian view of the trade cycle, according to Haberler (1932) 'bridged the gap between the monetary and non-monetary explanation(s)' of the phenomenon. Haberler argues that the pure monetary explanation (which he represents as the then British Treasury view) attributes the cycle to the injection of new money into the economy (either by a reduction of the banking system's interest rate—inducing people to borrow more—or by straight forward non-funding of government debt). Prices therefore tend to rise. Haberler points out that this explanation only illuminates why *price* cycles exist, not why employment cycles do:

Now, according to Mr Hawtrey (of the Treasury), there is a tendency in our banking system to keep the interest rate too low during the upward swing of the cycle; the prices rise, we get credit inflation, and sooner or later the banks are forced to take steps to protect their reserves—they increase the rate and being about the crisis and the depression.

Haberler then points out that the implication of the purely monetary explanation, if writers such as Hawtrey and Fisher, are accepted, is that all that would be required to avoid the cycle would be to maintain a stable price level. If the reason why banks or governments over-expand credit in expansionary times could be isolated, then this over-expansion could be avoided and so also the price cycles it initiates.

The purely monetary explanation, however, does not explain the *employment* cycle, nor why that cycle is more extreme in certain sections of the economy and less so in others. Haberler calls on Menger's insights of low order and high order goods, and the roundabout methods of production which imply more or less capital intensity. Haberler's terminology 'the vertical structure of production' is slightly different but the meaning is the same. He writes:

if, e.g., not much labour is used for lengthening the process and too small an amount for current consumption, we shall get a maladjustment of the vertical structure of production. And it can be shown that certain monetary influences, concretely, a credit expansion by the banks which lowers the rate of interest below that rate which would prevail, if only those sums, which are deliberately saved by the public from current income, come on the capital market—it can be shown that such an artificial decrease of the rate of interest will induce the business leaders to indulge in an excessive lengthening of the process of production, in other words, in overinvestments. As the finishing of a productive process takes a considerable period of time, it turns out only too late that these newly initiated processes are too long. A reaction is inevitably produced—how, we shall see at once—which raises the rate of interest again to its natural level or even higher. Then these new investments are no longer profitable, and it becomes impossible to finish the new roundabout ways of production. They have to be abandoned, and productive resources are returned to the older shorter methods of production. This process of adjustment of the vertical structure of production which necessarily implies the loss of large amounts of fixed capital which is invested in those longer processes and cannot be shifted, takes place during, and constitutes the essence of the period of depression.

When banks create credit, prices begin to rise because those firms who obtain the new money bid away factors of production from concerns engaged in producing consumer goods. Forced saving occurs. Wages and prices rise in high order industries and a restriction of consumption is imposed on those unable to increase their money incomes. The new money becomes income in the hands of the factors hired away from the lower stages. The recipients, adhering to *their* original saving: spending ratios will try to increase their absolute consumption. If they succeed then the proportions of the monetary flows in the economy going to each order of goods may be restored. This 'counter-tendency' can be overcome by further injections of credit but this process would lead to a continuously rising inflation rate which could not be persisted in indefinitely. When it ceases the more roundabout methods of production will no longer be able to continuously bid away real resources from low order production. These roundabout, capital intensive industries will have become unprofitable. They will be discontinued and the depression will commence.

Haberler (1932) then emphasises that if 'we accept the proposition that the productive apparatus (of the economy) is out of gear, *that great shifts of labour and capital are necessary* to restore equilibrium, then it is emphatically not true that the business cycle is a purely monetary phenomenon . . . although monetary forces have brought about the whole trouble. Since a dislocation of real physical capital . . . can in no case be cured in a very short time' (emphasis added).

Thus the pre-war Austrian view of the trade cycle differed from the early monetary approach (where only money mattered) and embraced 'real' factors as well. Because it included expectations it was relatively easy to reconcile it with the modern monetarist view of the vertically shifting Phillips curve. Because of its emphasis on both real and monetary variables it ran counter to Lord Keynes' recommendations and resulted in the great Hayek: Keynes debates of the 1930s.

Since it embraced the well-known fact that early boom is characterised by extensions in fixed capital, and that high order industries are the most volatile in boom and slump, it was at once both more acceptable as a theory to the non-monetarists of the day and less acceptable to Mr Keynes and his followers. This may appear paradoxical. But the paradox is resolved if we examine Keynes' recommendations to engage in public works as a cure for depression. In 1931 (p39) Keynes wrote 'No one believes that it will pay to electrify the railway system of Great Britain at 5% . . . At $3\frac{1}{2}\%$ it is impossible to dispute that it will be worthwhile. So it must be with endless other technical projects.'

If interest rates are pushed down for this purpose, however, the roundaboutness of production will certainly be increased and capital projects engaged in. And it is here that the Austrians departed from the Keynesian view. The Austrians emphasised that a reaction must inevitably set in if the expansion was not financed by real, voluntary saving rather than by credit creation.

Depression is the necessary and inevitable 'recovery' process of a government induced boom. Just as booms are marked by falls in the rate of interest, so they are characterised by a bidding-up of the prices of industrial goods relative to those of consumer goods and of commodity prices relative to those of industrial goods. So depressions see a fall in all prices with those furthest from the consumer falling fastest. As factors shift back to the lower orders of production some natural unemployment will occur. This will disappear provided real wage rates are not artificially high. From these insights we can move on to the modern Austrian view of stagflation.

Only a slight refinement is necessary. In essence all we need to bear in mind is that economics is concerned with relative price adjustments, not absolute movements. Hence the problem of stagflation—a slump with rising money prices. If government keeps on injecting money into the economy the adjustment between capital and consumer goods industries will still proceed. Hence the prices of consumer goods still rise relatively in a slump, but do so monetarily and absolutely as well. Government, by intervening in the economy's recovery process from the government-induced slump, has now 'deprived the public of the one great advantage of recessions: a falling cost of living' (Rothbard, 1975, Intro.). Not only that, but the recovery will be delayed. One of the most insidious effects of inflation is that it disguises price signals. Absolute price differentials are difficult enough for entrepreneurs (businessmen or consumers) to perceive but changes in the *rates* of price change, when most are changing and that upwards, given the countless goods involved, blur the signals of the market and so the wishes of consumers, to the detriment of their fulfillment.

The normative Austrian implication of this view of money and the trade cycle is that it suggests money, to quote Adam Ferguson out of context (*An Essay on the History of Human Society*, 1767), should originate as the 'result of human action, but not the execution of any human design'. Carl Menger (1976, p260) took the same stance, and explicitly referred to money, when he argued that individuals led by their own interests '*without agreement, without legislative compulsion, and even without regard to the public interest*' (emphasis in original) develop a means of exchange to facilitate trade. Mises formalised this in the regression theorem (p3 above).

Money includes (as a medium of exchange) not just cash but also money-substitutes (Mises, 1966, pp432–4). These can be sub-divided into money-certificates and fiduciary media. The former is identical to money and its owner can 'at every instant and free of expense' exchange it for money proper. Fractional reserve banking is not being practised. Changes in the quantity of money certificates do not alter the money supply nor play any role in determining the purchasing power of money.

Once fractional reserve banking is introduced, however, the supply of money substitutes will include fiduciary media. The ingenuity of bankers, other financial intermediaries and the endorsement and *guaranteeing of their activities by governments and central banks* has ensured that the quantity of fiat money is immense.

Is fiat money or fiduciary media worth the same as, say, money certificates or warehouse cash receipts of the same face value? One would think not. Under Gresham's Law 'bad money drives out good' when both circulate together. People hoard the good and try to repay debts in the debased currency. The least acceptable comes in time to set the exchange value of the whole currency in circulation. Others are withdrawn and put to higher valued uses (as for example have gold, silver and copper which are still seen daily by each of us, not as currency but as wedding rings or electric cables).

Apparently fiat money can be assessed at face value. But what is face value? In fact Gresham (as quoted) was wrong. Good money will drive out bad since debtors will not be foolish enough to accept fiat money with the indefinable face value of one pound (formerly of silver) or one dollar. However, if the debased currency or fiduciary media is 'legal tender', *if debtors are compelled by law to accept it*, then and only then is Gresham correct. The money is now a product of human design and not of human action.

Barry (1981, p21) points out that Austrians thus wish to 'depoliticise' money. Some, such as Mises advocate the use of a gold standard coupled with the abolition of central banking powers. Others, such as Hayek (1976) would agree with the latter suggestion but permit banks to produce money-substitutes linked to any commodities the individual bank saw fit. Since legal tender would cease to be meaningful under either schema, Gresham's Law would be invalid. (Although fiduciary media could still exist if bankers offered them and clients accepted them. But if central banking and the underwriting of commercial bank mismanagement was removed the 'fraction' in fractional reserve banking would be a very small component relative to what it is today).

Whatever method of currency backing was employed Austrians would be satisfied that the permanent inflationary threat of the government printing press had been removed (whether that printing press was used directly or via the fractional reserve system). Moreover the cause of the business cycle would also have been eliminated. As explained, an increase in the money supply is not 'neutral'. Everyone's cash balance does not increase uniformly as though money had been scattered evenly over the country. In the long run this is so, but only after the completion of the market process. Austrians maintain that study of this process is essential, not just the equilibria which (hypothetically) may exist at the beginning and end of the monetary injection. As we have noted, it is the *process* which explains the mal-investments which in turn explain the cycle. The Walrasian auctioneer does *not* attain instantaneous readjustments of price and interests levels due to an increased money supply, nor are these price adjustments uniform in direction or rate. As Barry (1981, p23) points out this is why 'sectoral unemployment can occur even if governments' followed Friedman's rule of a slow but steady rate of monetary expansion. In brief, Austrians do not disagree with monetarists that inflation is a monetary phenomenon—but because of their emphasis on the microfoundations of sectoral differences in the impact of money on the economy they view it as an even more potent factor.

Hence slump follows boom, but for a totally unnecessary reason: government inspired mal-investment. And the readjustment to 'normality' is more painful in terms of unemployment than it need have been: because although entrepreneurs could have and would have made mistakes they would not have done so simultaneously. Only some errors would have required correction. An error cluster only occurs when all entrepreneurs have received the wrong signals on potential profitability, and all have received the signals simultaneously through government interference with the money supply.

Thus we conclude with the observation we began with. Unemployment can only be persistently kept below some 'natural' level by an impossibly ever-accelerating inflation rate. The views of 'rational expectations' theorists that people will come to anticipate that inflation in advance can, of course, be reconciled with the notion of the neutrality of money expansion. For this to be valid empirically, however, the point of injection of the ever increasing additional money into the economy must always be the same *and* both the route and the rate whereby it passes through the economy must be identical on each occasion. Given changing individual tastes and technologies

Austrians find this view unacceptable. Rising prices would always change in their relative relationships.

In the next few pages we analyse this Austrian approach to macroeconomics, show how it can be contrasted with both conventional Keynesian and monetarist economics and thereby highlight the differences in the three approaches.

MODERN AUSTRIAN MACROECONOMICS

Roger Garrison (1978) has offered an intriguing exposition of how Austrian macroeconomics can be contrasted with standard Keynesian analysis. He does so without by-passing the problem of capital stock heterogeneity and he builds into his model the Austrian theory of interest (based on time preference) and of money as it effects the business cycle.

Garrison begins his exposition with the left hand panel of *Fig.* 4.1. This is a modification of Hayek's (1967, p39) production triangle. The production process begins at point T and proceeds leftwards until consumption goods valued at OY appear. Any point to the right of the origin and before T represents a position where either unfinished consumption goods exist (which will ultimately be valued at OY) or capital goods exist valued at the vertical distance from the

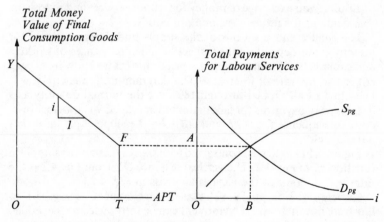

Figure 4.1

relevant point on *YF* to the *APT* axis (where *APT* is aggregate production time). The triangle represents 'all the various stages of production that coexist at each and every point in time' (Garrison, p173). The distance *TF* represents the value of the injection of labour into the production process. As the labour services grow in value until ultimately emerging as consumer goods worth *OY*, *FY* slopes upwards representing the increase in monetary value per unit of time per pound or dollar invested at *T*. Its slope is therefore 'the (simple) rate of interest (profit) when the economy is in equilibrium' (Garrison, p173).

Of course, in reality, as profit opportunities change capital and/or labour will be injected closer to *T* rather than *O* (or *vice versa*) thus lengthening (or shortening) the production structure. (At this point a fully employed economy is assumed thus it is the allocation of labour and capital along *APT* that has just been considered, not additional inputs.)

The right hand panel of *Fig.* 4.1 is the intertemporal market where the interest rate is determined. There the valuations of present and future goods are compared. The figure rests on the following premises:

(i) the supply of labour services (future consumption goods) is exchanged for money to demand presently existing consumption goods (D_{pg}) and

(ii) the supply of present consumption goods (S_{pg}) by capitalists results in an exchange of money for labour services and represents a demand for future consumption goods.

The shapes and positions of the supply and demand curves for present goods depend on the respective time preferences of workers and capitalists. The inter-temporal price ratio (as we know from page 66) is also the rate of interest, *i*. The diagram itself, has in *Fig.* 4.1, been first of all flipped through 180° over the normal quantity axis (total money payments for labour) and then rotated 90° anticlockwise. As a consequence $OA = TF$ and $OB = I =$ the slope of *FY* in the left hand panel.

Figure 4.1 can then be contrasted with the Keynesian consumption function as in *Fig.* 4.2. The vertical distance *OY* from *Fig.* 4.1 is the intersection point of the Keynesian cross in *Fig.* 4.2.

Garrison (1978, pp179–82) uses a development of *Fig.* 4.1 to illustrate how net capital investment can be introduced to the model. The structure of production will be lengthened as it becomes more

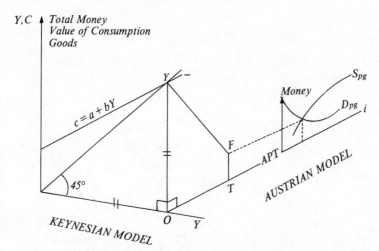

Figure 4.2

'roundabout'. The question is by how much? Figure 4.2 provides the answer. At this juncture we assume net investment can only come about by forfeited consumption not by credit creation. If this is so, then, in the left hand panel of *Fig.* 4.3 we can have two diagrams. The familiar structure of production diagram *OYFT* plotting total monetary consumption against *APT*, and a second pair of axes, with an origin of K_o, indicating zero net investment. K_o is horizontally opposite *Y*. As positive net investment occurs down the *I* axis *Y* will be reduced by the same monetary amount. In the panel the axes are drawn on the same scale so *I'* corresponds to net investment of $Y - Y'$ and so on. As *APT* is lengthened by positive net investment *OT* increases to *OT'* for net investment of *I'* and to *OT''* for net investment of *I''*. The line plotting the change in *APT*, $\Delta APT{:}I$ is of unknown shape but must have the positive direction indicated. Given that function, and given that ΔAPT is drawn on the same scale as *APT*, vertical lines can be dropped to *APT* to correspond to net investments of zero, *I'* and *I''*.

The right hand panel of *Fig.* 4.3 explains why these changes in investment have arisen. (The heavy lines in each panel come from *Fig.* 4.1) Individuals change their relative valuations of present as opposed to future goods. Thus a decrease in time preference by workers results in D_{pg} moving to D'_{pg}. The money values of present

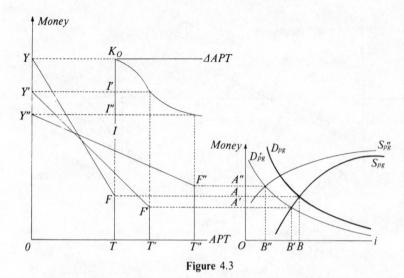

Figure 4.3

goods consumed and of wages paid out fall to OY'' and OA' respectively. Interest rates fall to OB' and net investment of I' occurs. The changed time preference of workers has released resources from current consumption. The accompanying decline in interest rates has made more time consuming methods of production attractive to capitalist entrepreneurs. And as Garrison (1978, p185) notes although money expenditure on final goods falls to OY', 'consumption in real terms decreases only temporarily and then rises to a new high once the additional investment comes to fruition'. The prices of consumption goods are thus pushed down by this extra supply emanating from the new investment to a level consistent with OY'.

A fall in capitalists' time preferences brings about similar results. The main differences are that S_{pg} shifts to S''_{pg}. The amount paid to workers, however, rises: from OA to OA''. But this is to be expected from the premises of page 70. The shift of S_{pg} is not only downwards, but is down and *to the right*. Thus capitalists pay more out for labour services representing their increased wish for higher real consumption in the future.

Figure 4.4 contrasts the Austrian and Keynesian models, where investment in the former is endogenous brought about by changing time preferences while in the latter it is exogenous.

78

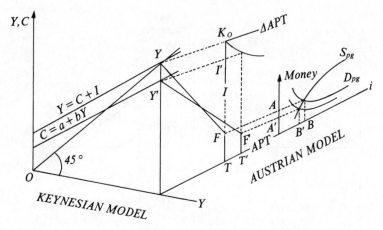

Figure 4.4

But what of money? We know that Austrians regard money as a critical determinant both of inflation and the trade cycle. We know they do not adopt the orthodox monetarist stance that money is injected uniformly throughout the economy. Garrison (1978, pp190–2) assumes for illustration, that given unchanged time and liquidity preferences an exogenous increase in the money supply will go first to capitalists, before percolating through the economy to other sectors such as workers. The top left hand panel of *Fig.* 4.5 illustrates the working out of these assumptions. The vertical axis, M_o represents any given original level of money stock. The horizontal axis represents the nominal magnitude of any given stock after an expansion has occurred. The 45° line shows where $M_o = M_e$ and would represent the impact of an expansion of the money stock. But if all the new money is extended as credit to capitalists and none to workers, then for any given M_o held by capitalists a new and higher M_e will be relevant. This is shown by the pivoting to the right of the 45° line to M_c'. Since labour is (initially) unaffected by the increased money supply the 45° line and M_L' remain identical. As capitalists purchase new quantities of labour services, however, the new money filters through the economy until the expansion experienced by both groups is approximately equal. This is shown by the movements of M_L' and M_c' to M_L'' and M_c'' respectively.

The consequence of this non-neutrality of monetary expansion is

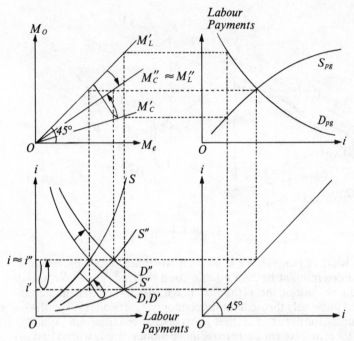

Figure 4.5

felt first of all in the market where present and future goods are traded. In terms of our earlier premises the supply of present goods falls down and to the right (and the purchase of labour services is increased). In the bottom left hand panel of *Fig.* 4.5 *S* shifts to *S'*. The interest rate consequently moves from *i* to *i'*. As the new money becomes more evenly spread, however, workers begin to demand more present goods and *D* (which stayed at *D* = *D'*) moves to *D''* and the supply curve shifts partially back to *S''*, while the interest rate returns to *i* (or *i''*).

Figure 4.5 has two right hand panels which correlate with the two left hand ones. The 'real' supply and demand curves in the intertemporal markets have remained unchanged during the monetary expansion. The rate of interest similarly is unaltered. This lack of change in real time preferences while action is in fact occurring based on misperceptions results, of course, in the mal-investments we

80

discussed in the previous section. These mal-investments must in turn be liquidated.

Figures 4.6 and 4.7 contrast the orthodox and the Austrian approach to monetary expansion. In *Fig.* 4.6 (Panels *IV* and *VI*) neutral (non-Austrian) monetary expansion occurs. (The monetary helicopter has dropped money evenly over all sectors of the economy.) No change occurs in the interest rate either temporarily or permanently (Panels *V* and *I*). No additional investment occurs. ΔAPT is zero. OT and OY remain the same. The only change which has occurred is that OY, in money terms, is now considerably larger

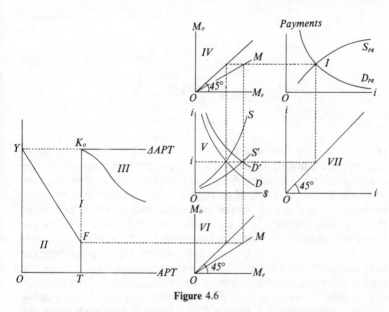

Figure 4.6

than before. (This effect is not shown in the diagram since Panel *VI* is similar but not identical to panel *IV*. It shows the monetary expansion but does not analyse where in the economy that expansion has occurred. It permits panels *II* and *III* to be compared with the remainder of the diagram in terms of M_o, the original money stock.)

Figure 4.7, however, includes a replication of *Fig.* 4.5 and shows how an expansion of the money stock goes in totality to capitalists

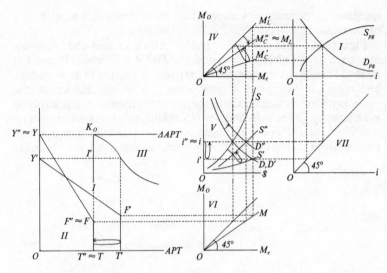

Figure 4.7

(Panel *IV*). This time the rate of interest falls (temporarily) to *i'*. Capitalists are misled into constructing new plant in areas which were not profitable before but now appear (falsely) to be so. The structure of production is lengthened to *OY'FT'*. This mal-investment must, however be liquidated as the increased money stock percolates through the economy. The additional investment K_oI' was not the result of voluntary saving. As Garrison (1978, p196) puts it 'the capitalists in their entrepreneurial roles bid labour . . . away from the later stages of production . . . and begin construction of . . . specific capital [equipment] to take advantage of the [apparent] profitability of . . . long[er] term projects. But in the very process of constructing . . . the newly created money flows from the capitalists to the labourers . . . whose tastes have remained unchanged, and who now have their full share of the new money, [they] bid for consumption goods in an amount consistent with the old . . . structure of production . . . Their time preferences have not changed. With their bidding for consumption goods the rate of interest rises . . . projects . . . are revealed to be unprofitable. Capitalists must act now to cut their losses.'

Garrison's arguments may seem still highly aggregative. They are.

82

But they are at a lower level of aggregation than those of non-Austrians. They are not the last word in Austrian macroeconomics. But they are consistent with Hayek's (1952, p31) statement that it 'is probably no exaggeration to say that every important advance in economic theory during the last one hundred years was a further step in the consistent application of subjectivism'.

REFERENCES

N P Barry, 'Austrian Economists on Money and Society', *National Westminster Bank Review*, (1981).

E Böhm-Bawerk, *The Exploitation Theory of Socialism–Communism*, (3rd rev edn), Libertarian Press, (1975).

R W Garrison, 'Austrian Macroeconomics: A Diagrammatical Explanation', in L M Spadaro (ed), *New Directions in Austrian Economics*, Sheed, Andrews and McMeel, (1978).

G Haberler, 'Money and the Business Cycle', in Quincy Wright (ed), *Gold and Monetary Stabilisation*, University of Chicago Press, (1932).

F A Hayek, *The Counter Revolution of Science*, Glencoe, (1952); 'Degrees of Explanation', (1955) reprinted from the *British Journal for the Philosophy of Science* in F A Hayek, *Studies in Philosophy Politics and Economics*, Routledge and Keagan Paul (1967); *Denationalisation of Money*, Institute of Economic Affairs, (1976); *Prices and Production*, Routledge and Kegan Paul; (1931); *The Constitution of Liberty*, Routledge and Kegan Paul, (1977); *A Tiger by the Tail*, Institute of Economic Affairs, (1978).

J R Hicks, *The Theory of Wages*, 2nd edn, Macmillan, (1963); 'Capital Controveries: Ancient and Modern', *American Economic Review*, (1974).

J M Keynes, *Unemployment as a World Problem*, University of Chicago Press, (1931); *The General Theory of Employment Interest and Money,* Macmillan, (1960).

I Kirzner, 'The Theory of Capital', in E G Dolan (ed), *The Foundation of Modern Austrian Economics*, Sheed and Ward, (1976); *Perception, Opportunity and Profit*, University of Chicago Press, (1979).

L M Lachmann, 'Towards a Critique of Macroeconomics' in E G Dolan *op. cit.* (1976a); 'On Austrian Capital Theory' in E G Dolan *op.cit.* (1976b).

C Menger, *Principles of Economics*, New York University, (1976).

L von Mises, *Human Action*, 3rd edn, Henry Regnery, (1966); *The Theory of Money and Credit*, Foundation for Economic Education, (1971); *Socialism*, Liberty Classics, (1981).

M Pirie, *The Logic of Economics*, Adam Smith Institute, (1982).

M Rothbard, *America's Great Depression*, Sheed and Ward (1975). 'Austrian Definitions of the Money Supply', in L M Spadaro, *op.cit.* (1978).
J Schumpeter, *A History of Economic Analysis*, Oxford University Press, (1954).

5 Modern Austrianism

In this chapter we return for the most part to the microfoundations of economics which the praxeological method of Austrianism is most obviously linked to. In turn we examine recent developments in the understanding of entrepreneurship, information, Schumpeterian innovation and managerial decision-taking in the presence of an uncertain future.

THE ENTREPRENEUR

A distinctive feature of Austrianism is that it views competition as a process not as a configuration of prices and quantities of different goods which, when mutually consistent define an equilibrium. We saw in Chapter 3 (p36) that one of the first modern economists to challenge this view was Hayek. Kirzner (1979, pp23–4) summarizes the Hayekian position thus:

(i) to understand each individual's plan, based on *his* knowledge and anticipations involves nothing more than the pure logic of choice
(ii) in disequilibrium individuals either cannot carry out their plans or will regret the fact that the outcome differs from that expected
(iii) a global set of mutually compatible plans requires again only the pure logic of choice for comprehension
(iv) the attempted execution by individuals of a set of mutually incompatible plans (incompatible because of ignorance or uncertainty) depends for its success (whether in whole or in part—a 'tendency towards equilibrium' as Hayek would put it) on the acquisition of relevant knowledge by and the dispelling of relevant uncertainty for the appropriate actors.

We further saw in Chapter 3 (pp35 and 40) that stage (iv) was simply 'assumed' by Hayek (at least from a praxeological stance). He explained lucidly the process of catallactics which brought it about with maximum economy of information (viz in his example of the

85

changing price of tin) but he did not provide a reason why a change in the supply of or demand for tin *would* be acted upon. Hayek saw price differentials primarily as efficient conveyors of information. As Kirzner pointed out (1979, p28) we have to turn to Mises and to praxeology to understand *why* and *when* the process of catallactics will be initiated in the presence of price differentials. This in turn leads into the study of the entrepreneur: a character relegated in most texts to the equivalent of a firm's top management (for example, Florence 1972 p197 and pp343–59) or mentioned only in a brief obeisance to Schumpeter (for example, Samuelson 1976 pp622 and 776) or, and very frequently, not mentioned at all (for example, Baumol 1972 and Koutsoyiannis 1979).

Since human beings act and since they do so in order to improve their current conditions there is a 'human propensity to sniff out opportunities lurking round the corner' (Kirzner, 1979, p29). As Kirzner hastens to point out, however, the exercise of entrepreneurial 'alertness' does not guarantee the discovery of all the relevant facts. Nor are the 'facts' uncovered and acted upon necessarily accurate; errors can occur. As we have already noted in Chapter 3, Mises emphasised that all action is speculative. The accomplishment of Hayek was to exorcise the careless use of the 'perfect knowledge' assumption from economic theory. Mises, and latterly Kirzner, have shown how Hayek's competitive market process (information dissemination and discovery) is set in motion by the entrepreneur. Whether any one entrepreneur or group is more effective than another, or whether any one environment is more conducive to effective entrepreneurship are, of course, still unanswered questions.

Nevertheless, 'within disequilibrium markets, the opportunities for gain that disequilibrium conditions themselves create (can be identified by the pure logic of choice). Postulating a tendency for such opportunities to be discovered and exploited, we can then explain the way . . . [this] . . . alters the pattern of opportunities presented in the market as the process unfolds' (Kirzner, 1979, p33).

If we turn to *Fig.* 3.2 (p45) we can obtain a flavour, not only of how entrepreneurs can bring buyer and seller together, but of how their arbitrage profit is whittled away by the competitive process. *Fig.* 5.1 is based on *Fig.* 3.2. Again we have two traders A and B, of goods X and Y, with initial endowments of E. We have already seen verbally (p48)

86

how one entrepreneurial middleman can bring A and B together, offer B more than his current marginal valuation of Y (in terms of X), and A more than his marginal valuation of X (in terms of Y given up). Absent transaction costs all three parties would end up better off, or, given transaction costs trade would take place provided the entrepreneurial profit was less than these costs.

Figure 5.1 assumes the presence of an entrepreneur who we will call a. As usual the possibilities for A and B to improve their positions are enclosed by the unlabelled indifference curves emanating from the respective origins. Entrepreneur a is alert to the fact that A and B are currently at point E and are unaware of any possibility of improving

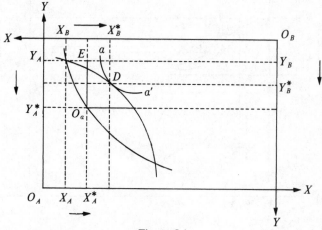

Figure 5.1

their positions. a knows (or thinks he knows) the preferences of A and B, he requires the quality of alertness, and simply offers A what he buys from B and *vice versa*. The preferences of a are indicated by (for example) the indifference curve aa' lying on a map emanating from the origin O_a, a mini-diagram with axes parallel to and of the same scale as the main figure. His optimal strategy is to move O_a along A's indifference curve until aa' is tangential to B's indifference curve at D. He then offers A just marginally more Xs than indicated by $X_A^* - X_A$ in exchange for a bundle of Ys just marginally less than indicated by $Y_A - Y_A^*$. B is offered just marginally more than $Y_B^* - Y_B$ in exchange for a bundle of Xs just marginally less than indicated by $X_B^* - X_B$. If we assume the marginal amounts required to induce A and B to trade with a are zero then the entrepreneur ends up at point D with a profit of Xs equal to $X_B^* - X_A^*$ and of Ys equal to $Y_A^* - Y_B^*$.

To introduce a competing entrepreneur, β, into the analysis we employ the same framework as in *Fig.* 5.1. The only difference in *Fig.* 5.2 is the introduction of an additional indifference map for β. $O\beta$ must lie on a higher indifference curve than A's original one in order

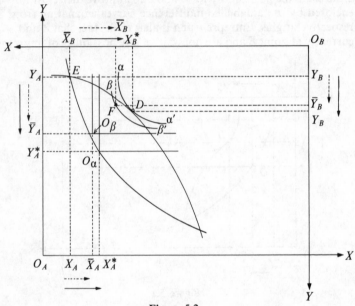

Figure 5.2

to encourage A to deal with β and not with a. Where a offered A $X_A^* - X_A$ in exchange for $Y_A - Y_A^*$, β offers fewer Xs but also obtains fewer Ys in exchange ($Y_A - \bar{Y}_A$ instead of $Y_A - Y_A^*$). Because of A's preferences this is a more favourable exchange and leaves him on a higher indifference curve at $O\beta$. Similarly B gives up fewer Xs ($X_B - \bar{X}_B$ instead of $X_B - X_B^*$) and gains fewer Ys ($\bar{Y}_B - Y_B$ instead of $Y_B^* - Y_B$) and the point F is more satisfactory to him than was D when he dealt with entrepreneur a. β is now making all the entrepreneurial profits, and not a. But these profits have been reduced from a's $X_B^* - X_A^*$ plus $Y_A^* - Y_B^*$ in *Fig.* 5.1 to β's $\bar{X}_B - \bar{X}_A$ plus $\bar{Y}_A - \bar{Y}_B$ in *Fig.* 5.2. It is difficult to see at first glance that β's profits are of necessity less than a's were, although *a priori* it must be so and geometric measurement would indicate it was. *Fig.* 5.3 abstracts from *Fig.* 5.2 the relevant indifference axes for a's and β's consumption of goods A and B. There it can be more clearly seen that a's consumption of both goods (i.e. a's profits) would be greater than β's consumption of both ($DH > FG$ and $KD > JF$).

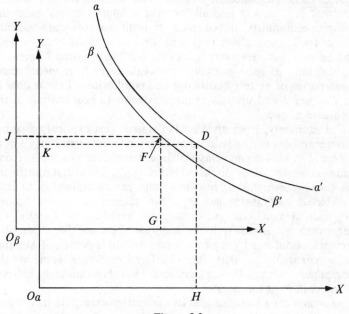

Figure 5.3

This diagrammatic discussion is a useful expository device although it does run the danger of being overly mechanistic. It suffers from the defect that disequilibrium is deemed always to be noticed by entrepreneurs. And, if this is the case, then entrepreneurship is something which can be readily specified and defined, and entrepreneurs are not then 'different' from any other type of person except in so far as their training and expertise differs: a lack of uniformity common to all human beings who follow varying careers with different preparatory backgrounds. On this view an entrepreneur is then no different than is a doctor, an engineer or a chemist from his fellow men. He has merely had different training from his fellows; as have his fellows from each other.

The above approach was developed in a recent and interesting book by Casson (1982). He defines the entrepreneur (p23) as '*someone who specialises in taking judgemental decisions about the coordination of scarce resources*' (emphasis in original). This definition enables Casson to concentrate on full-time, decision-taking managers (and not just on any and all 'purposive human actors' as would Austrian economists) in their role as co-ordinators of means and ends which are known, albeit only with probabilities of unity or less. Casson thus assumes away ignorance but the resulting framework enables him, at least partially, to break away from neoclassical assumptions of perfect knowledge and equilibrium. This he does in his Chapter 7 and usefully exploits Edgeworth box analysis of the kind used above.

Unfortunately, from an Austrian stance, this explicitly assumes that uncertainty can be reduced by a search for information (Casson, 1982, p119). This is a neo-classical development outwith the Austrian tradition which will be discussed below (p95). Second, it transforms the entrepreneur into a 'specialist' who can be trained or at least preselected and instructed into the science or art of 'taking judgemental decisions' with more or less success. Finally, the Edgeworth box is positively misleading in the sense that it describes entrepreneurial activity *ex post* whereas the whole essence of Austrian entrepreneurship is that the indifference curves seen by the entrepreneur are not those extant today but those which he believes *ex ante* will exist tomorrow.

Neo-classical economics and its derivatives exemplify this *ex post* inventory clerk approach. The inventory clerk looks at current consumption patterns, compares them with current productive capacity and concludes that the two do or do not arithmetically equate. In accordance with his policy preferences, he then advocates measures to maintain or remove any presumed mismatch of supplies and demands. The training of more 'specialists' who can take 'judgemental decisions' about coordinating scarce resources might be one such recommendation; the encouragement of increased search for extant information by existing, non-fully informed specialists might be another.

The Austrian economist does not prejudge the market in this way.

Demand patterns today do not necessarily represent what consumers want tomorrow. Likewise, an examination of physical manufacturing plant, research facilities and numbers and types of employees today does not necessarily indicate what industry can provide tomorrow. Only tomorrow's demand and supply behaviour can reveal that; and even then it can only do so in principle since in practice tomorrow's preferred supply and demand patterns will probably not achieve co-ordination or equilibrium. The Austrian economist does not presume to know before the event the most efficient way of producing a good. Nor does he presume to know in advance what the consumer will in fact want.

The Austrian economist does believe, however, that the entre-preneur believes that *he* knows. *A priori* this is true since the entrepreneur acts today as though he did, in fact, know. If the entrepreneur is right in his guess about tomorrow his actions will result in a profit, if not he bears a loss. Similarly the observer who takes the approach of the inventory clerk also believes he knows. If he is in a position to take decisions influencing tomorrow's market the results may also not reflect consumer and producer preferences. But the inventory clerk, and the politician who listens to him, unlike the entrepreneur, do not bear the full cost of their errors nor reap the full rewards of any correct assessments they may make. This has far reaching implications which will be discussed in Chapters 7 and 8 below.

To the extent that the entrepreneur is a 'specialist' who therefore can be trained to take 'decisions' he is simply the embodiment, as Florence (1972, p197) would have argued, of the firm's top management. A cynic might then claim, with some justice that the theory of the entrepreneur is 'all in Marshall'. He would, in fact be wrong.

At first glance, in Chapters vii and viii of Book VI of his *Principles* Marshall (1966) while discussing the 'undertaker' and manager of a business enterprise seems only to be preempting the hypothetical progress of Casson's (1982, pp1–6) Jack Brash. The 'undertaker' is described from his rise as a self-employed carpenter, through the role of a master-builder to a large scale businessman, to a manager of a joint stock company.

On closer inspection, however, Marshall's 'undertaker' is nearer in spirit to an Austrian entrepreneur than to any hypothetical business-man, however buccaneering. The rewards of Marshall's undertaker include and may be (or may not be) well in excess of the 'interest' on capital together with the earnings of the 'management' of that capital. To the extent that there is such a 'volatile' excess ('from a considerable negative to a large positive quantity' (p517)) it is due, according to Marshall, to a third component, namely the 'organisa- tion' which brought the first two, management and capital, together. This is *not* Cassonian entrepreneurship, (which rather is equivalent to Marshall's 'management'), but Marshall's 'organiser' *is* very close to the notion of the Austrian entrepreneur.

For example, Marshall, like Mises, emphasises the importance of speculative action as a cause of the organiser's (or entrepreneur's) profit: in 'trades in which the speculative element is not important . . . the earnings of management will follow pretty closely on the amount of work done in the business . . .' (p510). Here (ignoring the element of throwback to the labour theory of value) Marshall does not distinguish the 'management' task from the 'organisation' role so one could be accused of quoting out of context. Earlier, however, (p495) he points out that the 'gross earnings' of management is the reward accruing to both roles and the 'net earnings' of management is what accrues to 'organisation' alone. Marshall's terminology may not be of the clearest but his meaning is transparent.

The organiser is very close to the Kirznerian entrepreneur who earns his profit by discovering something obtainable for nothing at all (p52 above). As Marshall put it (p517) the organiser is alert to his opportunities if:

. . . profitable business opens out to him, [then] he regards the harvest accruing from it as almost pure gain; . . . . as a rule it scarcely occurs to him to set off his own extra labour as a deduction from these gains: they do not present themselves to his mind as to any considerable extent earnings purchased by extra fatigue . . . This fact is the chief cause . . . of the imperfect recognition by the general public, and even by some economists, of the . . . causes that determine . . . profits.

Of course, because of competition profit 'cannot long diverge from the normal supply price of . . . capital . . . added to the normal supply price . . . for managing . . .' (Marshall, 1966, p503). This view is perfectly compatible with the Austrian tradition and can be explained with the use of Edgeworth boxes as already illustrated. The potential of being misled by such expository devices has already been highlighted, however. The use of an *ex post* device to explain an *ex ante* activity has been amplified. A second drawback was mentioned when discussing Casson's definition of an entrepreneur as 'specialist' who takes 'judgemental decisions'. Marshall argues (p509) that this can encourage the observer to 'regard profits as remuneration of risk simply; . . . But this use of the term seems on the whole not advantageous, because it tends to class the work of management (here Marshall means 'gross' management including organisation) with mere routine superintendence.' Superintendents can, of course, be trained both in administration and actuarial risk assessment. They then become, as Casson would call them, 'specialists'. Marshall (p503) rejects this view. '[B]usiness power is highly non-specialised; because in the large majority of trades, technical knowledge and skill become everyday less important relatively to the broad and non-specialized faculties of judgement, promptness, resource, carefulness and steadfastness of purpose.'

Moreover, the Marshallian, speculative organiser, like the Kirznerian entrepreneur 'will reckon his labour . . . almost as nothing' (Marshall, 1966, p503). This is not the view of those who identify the entrepreneur with the specialist and trained manager 'whose services are scarce' and whose 'decision-making . . . [has] a positive opportunity cost' (Casson, 1982, p29).

It is then, the prospect of profit which praxeology informs us is the reason for catallactics in the presence of price differentials. The entrepreneur, on this view is seen primarily as an arbitrageur.

INFORMATION

The above discussion does *not* imply that the training of a specialist corporate manager is redundant. Nor does it suggest that the development of ever-more sophisticated decision-making tools is needless. What it does underline is that given ignorance about the future one cannot rely on the probabilistic approach of the trained administrator to initiate or react to future changes in an optimal fashion. First, his means of acquiring knowledge is costly and second, his knowledge acquisition (except in an evenly rotating, unchanging economy) will frequently be inappropriate. The latter is the more important reason since the normal calculus of marginal equivalency can be used to optimally overcome the former difficulty.

Table 5.1 encapsulates the argument to this point and illustrates how it will be developed in the pages below.

Table 5.1

The Acquisition of Knowledge		
Method		
1) Cost	Search Positive	Alertness Zero
2) Acquirer	Managers, corporate strategists, market researchers, research & development workers etc	Entrepreneur as arbitrageur
3) Parameters	The unknown is definable *ex ante* and its attainment is determined only by cost and apparent worth-whileness	The unknown is unknown *ex ante* and *ex post* awareness of it depends only on alertness to the existence of a hitherto unexploited opportunity
4) Returns and Private Objectives	Wages, interest, risk premia on capital employed, plus un-expected surpluses or deficits on computed returns due to un-anticipated changes occurring with the passage of time	Profits or losses to the extent that the entre-preneur's alertness was correct or inaccurate
5) Societal outcome	Facilitates tomorrow a deliberate move towards today's equilibrium	Permits a move today towards tomorrow's (perceived) equilibrium

The assumption of perfect knowledge is rarely claimed by any given economic writer to be one to which he intends to adhere. Nevertheless economists often either fail to drop the assumption or argue that information is, in fact, a free good. If this was indeed so then, of course, failure to discard the assumption would be valid. Stigler (1961) was one of the first to insist that the acquisition of knowledge in a (real) world of imperfect information is a costly process. He developed conventional theory to permit deliberate search behaviour. This allows transactors to make once-and-for-all exchanges at ruling equilibrium prices. Or, in the presence of imperfect information about the optimal equilibrium, time and effort and other costs can be incurred by transactors to find out the terms on which goods are available on the market. After a point, search will be abandoned in favour of purchase because the marginal costs of search themselves are about to exceed the marginal benefits of further search.

Alternatively, conventional theory permits transactors to take decisions using a wide variety of techniques developed explicitly to take account of different contingent outcomes (*see* Luce and Raiffa, 1957). Moreover, Bayesian decision theory enables transactors not only to take decisions using probability theory (prior analysis) but also enables them to collect further information and revise their probabilistic expectations in the light of information so acquired (posterior analysis).

But as Littlechild (1972, p7) points out, none of these elaborations on conventional theory meet the aim of understanding the market process:

[All of] these models more or less run down as the agents discover all there is to know . . . To see why this should be so, let us look more closely at the assumptions in the models. The agents are equipped with forecasting functions and decision functions to enable them to cope with uncertainty. Indeed the agents are these functions. But though their specific forecasts and decisions may change over time in response to changes in economic conditions, the *functions themselves remain the same.* The agents never learn to predict any better as a result of their experiences. Nothing can ever occur for which they are not prepared, nor can they ever initiate anything which is not preordained.' (Emphasis in original.)

Eventually they simply move towards and reach (at least in theory) the questionable Nirvana of equilibrium.

This type of knowledge acquisition via search implies that the information itself is to some extent already known (row 3, Table 5.1). As Boulding (1966) put it, there is a 'paradox . . . implicit in the very concept of knowledge . . . we have to know what we want to know before we can start looking for it'. If we want to reach the moon we must know in advance that certain avenues are open and others (for example, a sea journey) are closed. If we wish to produce a new mass market packaged food and to do so in a profit-maximising manner we must know how to undertake market research to spot market 'gaps', how to conduct dietary tests and kitchen development and how to ascertain the apparent profit-maximising price, promotion and product design package. A skilled judgemental decision-taker of the Casson mould is required plus expertise in these and other fields. (row 2, Table 5.1). And of course such resource owners must be rewarded (row 4). Part of the searching, even in this trite example, is to ascertain other people's plans (be they suppliers, competitors, or customers). Only if our food manufacturer can glean sufficient knowledge about them can he hope to take decisions which will be compatible with such plans and even permit equilibrium in principle. Unfortunately even if the searching were (impossibly) wholly exhaustive it would only reveal information about today on which tomorrow's decisions and actions would be based (row 5). The mirage of equilibrium would continue to recede.

None of this is to suggest that the literature on the economics of search is redundant. Rather it is to underline Kirzner's (1979, pp137–53) lament that it has diverted attention away from the acquisition of knowledge about which nothing is known at all. This type of knowledge is acquired without a deliberate plan and is composed of information spontaneously discovered. Such knowledge is not subject to the Boulding paradox that some prior information about the area must already be possessed. It is obtained not through a cost incurring deliberate search but *becomes* available at zero cost through the alertness of an entrepreneur spotting its potential value as a profit opportunity (rows 1 and 2, Table 5.1). It has a zero cost in the sense that no deliberate effort is made to acquire it (Kirzner, 1979, p143) but it is not a free good in the sense that all consume it (as with air) with no effort since only he who is alert 'consumes' or acquires such knowledge.

Nor is it a free good in the sense that if consumed the total stock is undiminished since once knowledge of a profit opportunity is acted upon other less alert entrepreneurs will also become aware and act upon it and the profit opportunity (and hence the information about it) will become progressively less as the market process unfolds. (Rows 3, 4 and 5). The information so acquired refers to a tomorrow. Once acquired (and acted upon) it progressively ceases to relate to an opportunity and increasingly becomes a part of history. As the 'consumption' of the knowledge good progresses the good changes form, and the stock of the original good becomes progressively less and less. Such a good is thus not a 'free good' as conventionally defined, despite its zero cost of acquisition.

This, of course, as we saw in *Figs*. 5.1, 5.2 and 5.3 is how the market process unfolds. Mutually beneficial exchange occurs between market participants. But the tendency towards (the ever receding) equilibrium illustrated there is brought about by the entrepreneur. As Kirzner (1979, pp150–1) puts it the market process translates

unnoticed opportunities for mutually profitable exchange . . . into forms that tend to excite the interest and alertness of those most likely to notice. . . . [w]here coordination has not occurred . . . this [is] an opportunity for pure entrepreneurial profit . . . [and] continued alertness to shifting opportunities . . . (is required) for continued spontaneous discovery . . . the market process [thus] disseminates knowledge whose very existence has not been known to its spontaneous learners.

Kirzner's view of knowledge, the two means of acquisition (search and alertness), and the importance of change develops, re-echoes and refines some of the concepts put forward earlier by Hayek (1945). The economic problem, he points out, is not how to allocate given resources but rather 'how to secure the best use of resources known to any of the members of society, for ends whose relative importance only these individuals know . . . It is a problem of the utilisation of knowledge which is not given to anyone in its totality.' Certainly there may well be a body of organised knowledge available to scientific experts. But as Hayek (1945) emphasises there is also a large body of non-scientific, unorganised knowledge of the specific 'circumstances of time and place'. Each 'individual has some advantage over all others with regard to this knowledge . . . [and] it is a curious fact that this sort of knowledge should today be generally regarded with a kind of contempt and that anyone who by such knowledge gains an advantage over somebody better equipped with theoretical or technical knowledge is thought to have acted almost disreputably.' Such knowledge, of course, can only be mobilised to provide the gains of trade if the individuals who 'possess' it are alert to the fact that it is there. Not only is this knowledge unique to the individual but it will remain unknown (even to him) unless he is stimulated to notice it.

What is this stimulus to alertness and how and why does it operate? The stimulus is perceived profit and the reason for its operation lies in the basic praxeological axiom given in p27 above. Man acts purposively to achieve goals which will leave him better off. His actions may or may not succeed in achieving the desired ends and the ends themselves, if achieved, may not, in the event, prove satisfactory. The fact that action takes time means that the future is unknown and that the actions chosen may turn out to have been inappropriate to achieve the desired ends if perceptions of future circumstances are wrong. Or the actions may be inappropriate because insufficient is known today about how to achieve tomorrow's desired goals even if the goals and their environment are correctly perceived.

With all of this uncertainty surrounding human action it might seem that there is seldom anything to be gained from action except the pleasures of the roulette wheel. Profits and losses could be argued to be randomly and fortuitously distributed. Yet any observer of economic life knows this is not the case. People do act. Risk preferrers do not make up an obvious and overwhelming majority of the human race. And although profits and losses do not always appear to go to the righteous and vicious respectively they frequently do go to those who satisfy or fail to satisfy a market demand. And with hindsight even loss makers can frequently be understood as those who acted to satisfy a market demand only to find that they had calculated or forecast that demand and the means of meeting it incorrectly.

In short, man acts and hence chooses, indicating his awareness of a divergence between tomorrow's situation as it will actually hold and tomorrow's situation as he foresees it. If this divergence did not exist he would have no need to act since the future foreseen would come about anyway. Purposive action then must be directed to the future as envisaged and not to the future as it will necessarily be realised. Since action is purposive and rational and directed to the envisaged future it follows that the action is directed to the aim of making the envisaged and realised futures correspond as closely as possible. Kirzner (1982, p149) calls 'this motivated propensity of man to formulate an image of the future *alertness*' (emphasis in original).

If this analysis of Kirznerian entrepreneurship (as explicated in 1982) is contrasted with Kirzner's earlier work (for example 1972) as summarised in Chapter 3 pp48–51 above then the contrast between Kirzner and Schumpeter is no longer as great as it was made out to be there. The 'early' Kirznerian entrepreneur was seen to be essentially an alert middleman who exercised an equilibrating force on a market forever in disequilibrium. Little attention was given by Kirzner as to why equilibrium should be 'ever receding'. For an understanding of that we had to turn to Schumpeter, who saw the entrepreneur primarily as a disequilibrating innovator. The two concepts differed. At a more generous level they were complementary. The new developments of Kirzner's thought, however, permit a reconciliation. He states (1982, p154):

... whereas in the case of entrepreneurship in the *single-period market* [that is ... the entrepreneur as arbitrageur] ... alertness meant alertness to present facts, in the case of *multi-period* entrepreneurship alertness must mean alertness to the future (emphases added).

Kirzner then reconciles both his original view of entrepreneurship with the Schumpeterian, and with the Hayekian definition of disequilibrium, particularly points ii and iv itemised on p85.

[The entrepreneur in the single period case is alert to the action he can take to prevent] transactions in different parts of today's market ... unconstrainedly diverg[ing] from being mutually inconsistent [and in the multiperiod case not only is this type of alertness present but so also is alertness] in the simple sense of ... awareness of the freedom with which his [the entrepreneur's] own envisaged future [concerning future market transactions] may diverge from the realised future. In particular the futurity that entrepreneurship must confront introduces the possibility that the entrepreneur may, by his own creative actions, in fact *construct* the future as *he* wishes it to be. In the single period alertness ... at best discover[s] hitherto overlooked current facts. In the multiperiod case ... alertness must include the ... perception of the way in which creative and imaginative action may vitally shape the kind of transactions that will be entered into in [the] future ... [this] alertness ... will indeed call for personal and psychological qualifications that were unneeded in the single period case. To be a successful entrepreneur one must now possess ... qualities of vision, boldness, determination and creativity ... [rather than ... merely [being the first person to see] that which stares one in the face] ... However, the function ... in the multiperiod context [remains the same. Entrepreneurship] accomplishes ... a tendency for transactions in different parts of the market [including the market at different dates] to become coordinated. The incentive [remains] the lure of pure profit.' (Kirzner, 1982, pp154–5).

This development of Austrian entrepreneurial theory brings Kirzner, and Schumpeter much closer together yet does so without sacrificing the essential views expounded by Hayek, Mises and Kirzner that what is important about perfectly competitive equilibrium as an analytic tool is not the state it describes, but the real world tendency to move towards that state. It also enables Schumpeter's innovator/entrepreneur to be fully embraced in the Austrian mainstream rather than allowing his valuable contributions to be appended as interesting asides, or neglected entirely as being incompatible with neo-classical static equilibrium theory.

SCHUMPETER'S ENTREPRENEUR REVISITED: A DIGRESSION

Although Schumpeter was originally a pupil of Böhm-Bawerk and Wieser in Vienna and although a system of equilibrium analysis never appealed to his intellect he has never been wholeheartedly accepted by the Austrian School. In this current chapter, however, we have attempted to show that the alleged differences between the Schumpeterian view of the entrepreneur and the Mises: Kirznerian approach have possibly been more apparent than real. It would be less easy and probably incorrect, on the other hand, to reconcile the Misesian and Schumpeterian view on the causes of the business cycle (monetary fluctuations and mal-investment in the former case and multiperiod entrepreneurship in the latter). In this section we will concentrate on these similarities in the interpretation of the entrepreneur and the competitive process and not on Schumpeter's views of the macroeconomic scene where at present it is still difficult to see how he can readily be re-embraced into the Austrian fold.

Schumpeter defined innovation to include not only the introduction of new products and new techniques of production, but also the opening up of new markets and supply sources, the improvement of management techniques and the introduction of new distributive methods. The person responsible for doing these and other 'different things' was the entrepreneur. He was the individual who was, in Kirzner's wording, trying to 'construct the future'.

This is not to suggest that technical change only entered economic discussion with Schumpeter. Adam Smith's division of labour not only raised the productivity of the pin-makers but encouraged them to seek for new technologies and the 'invention of a great number of machines . . . by which labour is so much facilitated and abridged' (Smith, 1776, pp112–4). Other classical economists such as Ricardo also acknowledged the impact of 'technical progress' on economic growth. To Ricardo (1821, chapter 31) the introduction of new machinery lowered production costs. These would benefit the producer by generating unusual profits which would persist until others adopted similar methods, thus competing away the profits and so benefiting the consumer through lower prices as a result of competition. Ricardo tended also to argue (chapter 6) from the assumption that real wages would never rise above a 'natural' subsistence level. Nominal wages would vary with the price of necessities (such as food and clothing) whose prices in turn would be subject to upward pressure due to the impact of diminishing returns to land. Ricardo thus saw two opposing forces at work, diminishing returns causing prices to rise, and technical progress which would encourage them to fall.

This is in general agreement with Smith (1776, p111) who, while optimistic about the possibilities of the division of labour believed that its potential was limited mainly to the then small sector of 'manufacture' rather than the predominant sector of 'agriculture'. Ricardo concurred with this and gloomily prophesied that the introduction of machines in agriculture would be insufficient to offset the trend of rising prices. The rising prices of necessities would force the nominal wage level up, capitalists' corresponding profits would decrease and hence 'the motive for accumulation ceases' (1821, chapter 21).

Thus while the classical economists were not unaware of the importance of technical progress for prompting economic growth, they appear to have considered the limited resource of land as having an equal if not greater negative influence. This relegation of innovation was reinforced by the development of non-Austrian marginalism and neo-classical economics. The development of the concepts of consumers' and producers' equilibria required a static framework with preferences and technology taken as givens.

Schmookler (1965) argues that this led to a blindspot in economics which lasted for several decades. The analytic convenience of a given production function with isoquants everywhere convex to the origin implied that higher output could only be obtained by an increase in either labour or capital permitting movement to a higher isoquant. With full employment and a fixed labour supply, however, ever increasing inputs of capital while increasing output, would result in a diminishing marginal physical product of capital and a Ricardian decrease in 'the motive for accumulation'.

A paper by Abramowitz (1956), which suggested that by far the greatest part of American economic growth between 1874 and 1953 was due to an unexpected 'residual' factor, not labour or capital, challenged this view. This 'residual' was hypothesised to be the increase in the stock of and use of technical know-how. In short, innovation was continuously moving the entire production surface up and to the right. This documented finding resulted in what Nelson (1962, p4) called a 'renaissance of Schumpeter'.

Two points are worth making here. First, the importance of technological progress was *not* disregarded between the phasing out of the Classical School, to reappear briefly with Schumpeter, and then vanish again into oblivion until Abramowitz's work. Second, to the extent that a 'renaissance' has come about in conventional economics it has rather been by way of an attempt to graft innovation on to the well-developed static neo-classical framework and has not been by a return to a study of the market process as understood by economists from Ricardo through Schumpeter and Mises to modern Austrianism.

The disregard of innovation by the neo-classicals in the Walrasian and Paretian tradition of marginal analysis has already been established by citing a (very brief but typical) selection of their own admissions. Menger and the Austrian marginalists, however did not neglect innovation so blatantly. Menger (1976, pp67–74) builds directly on Smith and the Division of Labour and incorporates the concept of capital intensive production using his own terminology of 'higher' and 'lower order goods'. 'In its most primitive form, a collecting economy is confined to gathering those goods of lowest order . . . offered by nature.' When specialisation and technical change occurs

men abandon this . . . [and] *investigate the ways* in which things may be combined in a causal process for the production of consumption goods, take possession of things capable of being so combined, and *treat them as goods of higher order*, they will obtain consumption goods that are as truly the results of natural processes as [the primitive] economy, but the *available quantities* of these goods *will no longer be independent of the wishes and needs of men*. Instead . . . they will be determined by a process that is in the power of man and is regulated by human purposes within the limits set by natural laws. (emphasis added).

Here Menger is giving us a definition of the industrial research and development laboratory six years before Edison had constructed his 'scientific village' and invention factory at Menlo Park. Interestingly, Menger lists as examples of innovation agricultural chemicals and fertilisers, and, at least by implication, is thus less concerned than Smith that agriculture would not provide the scope for technical change that manufacture could. Menger concludes that '[n]othing is more certain than that the degree of economic progress of mankind will still, in future epochs, be commensurate with the degree of progress of human knowledge.'

While Menger, Schumpeter and Mises did not neglect technological progress, the Paretian neo-classicists did. What was so compelling about Schumpeter's discussion that the 'so-called' renaissance occurred? And why has that renewed interest in innovation failed to bring Austrianism and the neo-classical orthodoxy closer together? The reason, already suggested, is that the Schumpeterian analysis was too dynamic to be grafted on to the static framework of equilibrium (or even on to such refinements as comparative static analyses).

In *Business Cycles* (1939) Schumpeter distinguishes between the innovator and the inventor. His entrepreneur is the former and the two roles will rarely, he argues, be combined. He assumes that innovations require 'New Plant', operated in 'New Firms' established for the purpose, accompanied by the coming to the fore of 'New Men', the entrepreneurs who will manage the New Firms. These are assumptions about which 'there is no lack of realism' (p96). Later, however, Schumpeter modified some of those views, particularly with regard to New Men and New Firms:

This social function [entrepreneurship] is already losing its importance . . . innovation itself is being reduced to routine. Technological progress is increasingly becoming the business of teams of trained specialists who turn out what is required and make it work in predictable ways . . . (Schumpeter, 1942, p132).

This, of course, is little different from Menger's ideas except that Schumpeter is rather more humanly confident. Menger placed a limit on progress 'set by natural laws'. Schumpeter, here is almost raising man above nature. Moreover, Schumpeter, in his desire to drop his earlier assumption about New Men in favour of research teams is no doubt at least partly correct, but, short of ascribing to such teams a supra-natural ability, it seems a *non-sequitur* to argue that entrepreneurship is thus no longer important. Schumpeter had come to agree with Mises that entrepreneurship is primarily a 'function not a man' but in so doing he belittled the function. Mises (1963, pp252–3) argues that economics 'in speaking of entrepreneurs, has in view not men, but a definite function. This function . . . is inherent in every action.' And of course, (p252) 'action is always uncertain', it is always speculative.

Like Ricardo's businessman, Schumpeter's entrepreneur earns a profit but these are quickly removed by the competitive process. Or, as Schumpeter put it rather more picturesquely, they are washed away by the 'Perennial Gale of Creative Destruction'. Should this perennial gale appear too quickly or blow too strongly profits will fall to levels discouraging further innovative activity. In the language of neo-classical economics a monopoly or imperfectly competitive position can give entrepreneurial profits protection and so in the long run encourage more expansion than any accompanying restriction of output and pricing above marginal cost levels will cause in the conventional analysis. As Schumpeter pithily puts it 'cars are travelling faster . . . because they are provided with brakes' (1942, p88).

Schumpeter thus discounts the dangers generally attributed to monopoly in the static Structure: Conduct: Performance (S:C:P) model of industrial economics. (The S:C:P: paradigm is simply the name given to that development of Paretian optimality relevant to the economics of industry, (Reekie, 1978)). Rather he believes most monopoly positions will be used to facilitate and encourage innovation. Monopoly market power will bring the necessary protection from the perennial gale and the size of firm implied by such market power will enable the resources to be generated to fund innovative and entrepreneurial activity: to 'construct the future' as Kirzner would put it.

This says Schumpeter, is the kind of competition 'which counts':

the competition from the new commodity, the new technology, the new source of supply, the new type of organisation . . . competition which commands a decisive cost or quality advantage and which strikes not at the margins of profits and the output of the existing firms but at their foundations and their very lives. (1942, p84).

Here Schumpeter also departs from both Austrians and neo-classicists and lays much less emphasis on price as a conveyor of information to either market participants or outside observers. Stable money prices do not, he argues, necessarily indicate lack of the 'competition which counts' since product improvement may indicate a falling real price for any given product service rendered.

Schumpeter's views have since been tested in numerous industries and economies. The basic questions asked generally being: do larger firms perform more R&D (Research and Development) than small, other things equal. Are larger R&D efforts more productive than smaller? Are Schumpeter's implied relationships continuous or is there, as Markham (1965) argued Schumpeter meant, only a minimum threshold size of firm and R&D effort up to which the Schumpeterian relationship holds? More recently Nelson and Winter (1978) have developed a quasi-Schumpeterian view still further arguing that Schumpeterian competition provides winners and losers, but the nature of the process is such that the winners become ever more successful which results in ever increasing industrial concentration.

The earlier tests of the Schumpeterian hypothesis provided results which varied (not unexpectedly) by industry and by time (i.e. as factors peculiar to any given industry altered). This is not surprising. The normative framework within which they were carried out, however, was always that of neo-classical analysis: that some deadweight loss due to monopoly behaviour was the price which society must pay for innovation. This is, of course, a false view. As Littlechild (1981) points out, such a deadweight loss is wholly in the eye of the beholder. 'The *relevant* alternative is (not perfect competition but) for the good *not to be supplied at all*.' (emphasis in original) Since it is produced, the entrepreneur's action is pure social gain equal to the producer's plus consumers' surpluses to which production and consumption of the innovation has given rise. (In *Fig.* 5.4 Littlechild argues this is $\pi + S$, not $\varDelta$.)

The Nelson and Winter variant of Schumpeter, based on a stochastic computer simulation model, is a plausible extension of an evenly rotating economy which is subject to a shock and allowed to recover. It is far removed from that level of continuous, ever changing, speculative human actions which is inherently unpredictable and continuously unstable.

In short, Schumpeter has, as mentioned earlier succeeded, after a period of neglect, in re-obtaining attention from some non-Austrian economists. Entrepreneurship has again come to be seen as

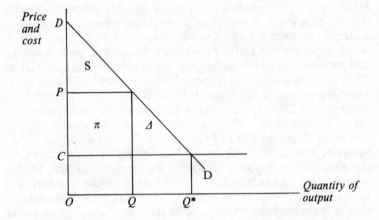

The conventional welfare loss due to monopoly. *DD*, Demand function, *P*, monopoly price; *C*, unit cost (including cost of capital); π, profit (above normal return on capital); *S*, consumer surplus; *Δ*, welfare triangle. *Source:* Littlechild (1981), *op. cit.*

Figure 5.4

important. But those economists who have taken note of this 'renaissance' have limited their overall vision to the existing neo-classical framework and either tried to assess empirically whether Schumpeterian entrepreneurship (as gauged by some form of R&D input or output) is or is not correlated with certain types of static market structure. Still fewer economists have extended Schumpeter's views on a dynamic front; they have done so using mechanistic models, which even if updated with new information as it appears, do not take account of the unknowable and unpredictable of which the entrepreneur, by definition is a provider. Schumpeterian thought could yet provide a bridge between Austrianism and mainstream economists but although the potential is present the neo-classical writers still seem to be too firmly wedded to the concept of static, knowledgable equilibrium or its derivatives for this to be other than a distant hope.

THE MULTIPERIOD AND THE HAYEKIAN TRIANGLE ONCE MORE

As long ago as 1870, Menger (1981, p69) pointed out that a 'person with consumption goods directly at his disposal is *certain* (emphasis added) of their quantity and quality.' But we have already seen (p102 above) that Menger argued that increased welfare depends on production and exchange of higher order goods. A person in command of such higher order goods only has 'indirect command' (p69) of the lowest order consumption good and he 'cannot determine with the same certainty the quantity and quality of the goods of first order that will be at his disposal at the end of the production process'. The nature of the uncertainty says Menger (p70) is partly dependent on the nature of the goods themselves and of the production process but it is also partly due to other elements 'of such a kind that we have not [yet] recognised their causal connection with our well-being', and partly it is due to factors whose influence we can understand but cannot control. The former is progressively reducible through search and alertness and Menger gives an example of knowledge of soil type and its relationship with plant growth. The latter, conversely, is understood but uncontrollable, and here Menger uses the example of the effect of weather on a harvest. (Menger's general point is taken, although in his specific example an alert entrepreneur might well shift geographic location so that climate would, if not become more predictable, at least become less surprise prone.)

These comments enable us to reintroduce the Hayekian triangle and see how the progression from higher to lower order goods in the presence of incomplete knowledge has *not* been disregarded by some writers in the field of modern business management. In particular Alderson (in marketing) and Shackle (in finance and investment appraisal) have come remarkably close to being intellectual heirs of the original Austrians, although the former in particular tends to have been neglected by modern day Austrians (Reekie and Savitt, 1982).

In the next few paragraphs we will examine some of the contributions of these two writers.

Alderson
Alderson attacked the problems of the market from the point of

view of the businessman who requires knowledge of *how* markets operate (and recommendations of how they may be made to work better). Alderson did not believe that general equilibrium analysis could provide sufficient understanding of the market process: hence, he argued that such an approach must be widely expanded. 'Economics as the mathematical logic of scarcity is invaluable for marketers but not sufficient. . . . But the level of taste, the technological functions, and the *flows of information* which the economist takes for granted are the primary business of a science of marketing' (Alderson, 1965, p303, emphasis added). This is similar to the view Austrian economists expressed. '[F]aulty decision-making is [more than] mistakes in arithmetic. . . . [m]aking the 'right' decision . . . calls for a shrewd and wise assessment of the realities [both present and future] within the context of which the decision must be taken' (Kirzner, 1980, pp6–7).

Alderson also emphasised the primacy of the *ex ante* entrepreneurial element in decision-taking. Decisions in real life are taken today with a view to affecting conditions tomorrow. This in turn implies that decisions must be taken without full information and that the consequences can result in either gains of losses for the decision-taker. To the extent that he 'guesses right' he makes profits. If he 'makes mistakes' he incurs losses. The profits from guessing right persist only so long as other market participants do not emulate him.

Alderson's theory of market behaviour begins by stripping away the assumptions of economic theory. He does this in several ways. His taxonomy replaced homogeneity with heterogeneity. Heterogeneity means that buyers have an infinite range of demands. It also means that the total set of wants is unique for each individual. Because such demands are heterogeneous suppliers in their turn may satisfy them in an infinite number of ways, subject to more or less accurate perceptions of the differences. Hence, simplified concepts of supply and demand have little explanatory value since they ignore the diversity of the real world. The *attainment* of equilibrium is unimportant to Alderson. The attempt to reach it is.

Alderson broadened the concept of demand by focusing on the desired attributes of each of a bundle of items. This makes the consumer's matching process complex. The value of the assortment sought by a demander can be described in terms of potency.

Potency . . . [is] the probability that the assortment will prove adequate . . . over a planning period. The rational justification for buying [a] product . . . is that it will narrow the gap between the potency of some ideal assortment and [that of] the actual assortment as it will stand after the purchase . . . (Alderson, 1965, p132).

That is, a motivating force for the demander is increased potency or, to put it another way, it is the anticipated achievement of a differential advantage in assortments. Creation of, or search for, this differential advantage is the engine of change on the supply side (Alderson, 1965, p29).

Alderson's concept of supply rejected traditional market morphology because aggregate supply is laid out in terms of a homogeneous demand. In the perfectly heterogeneous market, 'each market segment of demand can be satisfied by just one unique segment of supply' (Alderson, 1965, p29). Hence, it is artificial to link firms together just because they produce similar products since they are actually serving different markets. Competition should not be defined in traditional market structure or S:C:P terms but the emphasis should be shifted to the creation of differential advantage by individual firms in their pursuit of markets. Firms can rarely be sure what price is 'right' nor what product offering is 'right'. They must seek the answer in markets which are usually open to entry from competing suppliers. Alderson stresses that firms actively strive to secure a 'unique niche' in the market in pursuit of profits. This competitive striving, however, is taking place, by definition *before* the unique niche is attained.

The search for differential advantage is based on *expectations* about demand. The degree to which a market position can be maintained once attained, is the degree to which it continues to be successful in matching supply and demand. *Ex post* the industrial economist's traditional inclination has been to say that this is the essence of monopoly but the true meaning is exactly the opposite. The ability to find and hold a segment is indicative of competition through successful *ex ante* entrepreneurship. The firm has worked through the informational complexities of the market process. Tastes change, demanders change potency requirements, and some suppliers react. As supply conditions change, other suppliers in their turn, offer new goods and information. In short, the market becomes still more heterogeneous. But the knowledge that this is so increases the problem of matching supply with demand. The statement that, 'the heterogeneous market can only be cleared by information' (Alderson, 1965, p30) is Alderson's acknowledgement of this. The transaction costs of mutually beneficial exchange (information provision and search and sorting costs) have increased.

What does this imply? Both tangible and intangible goods (information) must pass through what Alderson called the sorting process. This involves the transformation of supplies from raw inputs which fail to meet demand into assortments of finished goods which can satisfy wants. (This, of course, is simply Menger's movement from higher to lower order goods. There is no written evidence that Alderson had read Menger). Thus exchange can take place creating want satisfaction for both parties. In order for transactions to occur gaps between buyers and sellers and their respective desires and offerings must be bridged. The gaps are those of space, time, technology, form, and most importantly, information.

Want satisfaction in marketing is a much more complex concept than that presented by the interaction of supply and demand curves. Exchange can take place when there is minimum want satisfaction for either participant; in other words partial congruence of supply and demand is necessary and sufficient to indicate that a transaction has been, or can be, successful. Total congruence is also sufficient, but it is unnecessary and, indeed, implausible. (Although the closer to perfect congruence the market process approaches the higher, for a time, will be some suppliers' profits and the greater, for a period, will be some demanders' satisfaction.) It is more appropriate to speak of partial congruence among the various elements in an offering set (O) and a demand set (D) such as:

$$O_1, O_2, \ldots, O_4, \ldots, O_6, \ldots, O_n$$

$$D_1, \ldots, D_3, \ldots, D_6, \ldots, D_8, \ldots, D_n$$

The presence of discrepancies between offering characteristics and demand characteristics, satisfaction available and satisfaction wanted, indicates opportunities for entrepreneurial activities. Such opportunities are grasped by conducting the sorting process (Narver and Savitt, 1971, pp64–66).

The sorting process has four stages. First, sorting out represents the breaking down of heterogeneous collections into homogeneous sub-lots to take advantage of economies of production or handling.

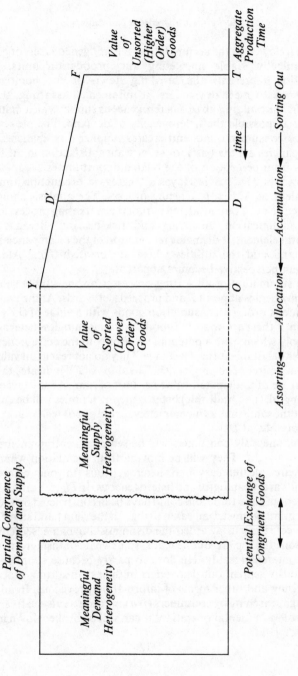

Figure 5.5

This is followed by the accumulation of homogeneous sets of goods in economically viable marketing and production units. Third, allocation represents the breaking down of the homogeneous collections to meet demanders' requirements. Assorting, the final stage, is the building up of a heterogeneous supply which matches as closely as possible the heterogeneity of demand. The process both satisfies consumer wants and creates supplier discrepancies. These discrepancies are the basis for seller want satisfaction in the form of profits from perception of the related opportunities.

Shown in *Fig.* 5.5 is Hayek's 'aggregate production time', the equivalent of Alderson's sorting process. The analysis shows how production must be considered part of the marketing process as much as communication, financing and risk-bearing. Because of its temporal element, it demands recognition of the discrepancies which are found and the utilities which are created. Thus Alderson's Austrian perspective becomes apparent.

The summation of all sorting processes on the supply side of an economy begins at point *T* and proceeds leftwards. At the end of this continuous process, consumption goods with a value of *OY* emerge. At point *T* there are no sorted goods only a meaningless heterogeneity of supply which have a potential value only to the entrepreneur who foresees profitable future exchange. They do not reach full value until the completion of sorting at *OY*. The slope of *FY* indicates their rate of increase of anticipated value per unit of time. At any given point, meaningful, (i.e., tradeable) heterogeneous supplies will be emerging at O at the same time as incompletely sorted goods will be in existence (for example, at *DD*[1]).

Simultaneously consumers will be searching entrepreneurially in their own right. They will be moving from a situation where their wants are meaningless and heterogeneous to one where their demands are meaningful and heterogeneous. In *Fig.* 5.5 an Aggregate Production Time trapezoid could have been constructed on the left of the diagram symmetrically akin to that on the right hand side. Sorting by the consumer is awarded the distinguishing name 'searching' by Alderson (1965, p36). But he tends, somewhat confusingly, to use the words interchangeably. He does so partly because suppliers often 'vicariously search' out demanders in their own sorting process (by advertising and other forms of information provision). In addition, although searching by consumers *vis a vis* producers is relatively more often solely 'a mental operation' it can still be broken down into the four sorting stages. 'Sorts are performed in selecting the [items] which can best be added to the consumer's [basket of wants]' (Alderson, 1965, p36).

Decisions made at T on the Aggregate Production Time function are made on assumptions about demander expectations at the time the goods will be in the assorting stage. Given the changing nature of demand sets, there is no assurance that more than partial congruence will result.

Since the process is time, space, form and technologically dependent, there are bound to be discrepancies, as noted previously. For the sorting process to operate, whether at a macro or at a micro level, information must be generated and received by suppliers and demanders at each stage of the process. The critical question is 'How much information is enough?' Market clearance, the partial intersection of the two heterogeneous demand and supply sets comes about only through the creation, dissemination and reception of information. The greater the congruence achieved, *ex post*, the greater the profitability of the supplier, the greater the want satisfaction of the consumer. *Ex ante*, however, as noted, full congruence is unlikely. Nevertheless, the task of the entrepreneur (prior to sorting or its completion) is to maximise this expected level of congruence.

Alderson's view that markets can achieve partial want satisfaction only through the production, dissemination and reception of some optimum quantity of information has been considered by economists concentrating on the economics of search. Yet in so doing they ignored alertness and failed to emphasise that risk, uncertainty and ignorance are three different concepts.

Stigler and others deal skilfully with risk and uncertainty. Ignorance, however, is almost totally neglected. Risk represents a condition where all possible states of the future are assumed known and a probability distribution can be defined for those states. With this data the economist can forecast the equilibrium using the expected value criterion. The analysis of resource allocation can then proceed in the normal manner. When uncertainty is present, all possible outcomes are again known but there are numerous probability distributions with associated subjective weights.

In reality such a full list never is available. This is Loasby's (1976, pp7–9) state of 'partial ignorance'. In such a state general equilibrium analysis and decision-taking by purely mathematical techniques is impossible. Managers must seek to overcome 'information mismatch' or ignorance without relying on expected value calculations, either objectively or subjectively constructed (Alderson, 1965, pp60–64). A product is only 'adequately identified' for a consumer (i.e., the optimal information is provided) if, in his ignorance 'the supplier has guessed right' (Alderson, 1965, p61). 'Guessing' of course, is simply a way of overcoming ignorance. It is not a computative process; it is intuitive. It is the process of entrepreneurship in which the successful guesser or entrepreneur makes a profit, the unsuccessful a loss.

This entrepreneurial perspective places Alderson directly in the mainstream of Austrian economics. The greater the thrust toward heterogeneity on the part of the demanders and the greater the attempts to satisfy it by suppliers (alertness and constructing the future), the more difficult and important the role of the decision-maker becomes. The decision-maker is faced with the ever increasing importance of ignorance which simultaneously offers difficulties and opportunities in achieving exchange. By contrast the manager in a controlled economy, or in a textbook perfect market is not confronted by this since ignorance and heterogeneity are either ignored or not fully recognised. In the transition from the homogeneous market, (which is either directed or automatically moved to equilibrium through adjustments in price or quantity) to discrepant markets, which are persistently radical and never static, entrepreneurship replaces bureaucratic management. Alderson indicated this and even identified the ever-receding nature of equilibrium:

A homogeneous market can be cleared by adjustments of price and quality. A heterogeneous market is cleared by information matching two sets, one ranging over heterogeneous demand and the other over heterogeneous supply. A discrepant market can only be cleared by innovation. . . . If strongly motivated problem solvers face each other . . . it can never be cleared but only moves in the direction of that equilibrium state. Another state, representing new requirements and new opportunities, has arisen before the last is satisfied (Alderson, 1965, p207).

Alderson pointed the way to the study of the successful 'guesser' or entrepreneur. He wished to see the 'theory of markets' and not the 'theory of resource allocation' at centre stage. The process of exchange, not the computation of marginal rates of substitution, is the purpose of a market.

We are ignorant of exchange possibilities because we are dealing with other humans. Robinson Crusoe could rely on static marginal equivalency as his guiding principle but whenever Man Friday came on the scene, inter-personal association and trade were inevitable. The motivations of each to trade were the obvious ones of moving from less preferred to more preferred positions, and doing so voluntarily. But neither Friday nor Crusoe knew what the other had to offer, and even if they (impossibly) did know what the other has to offer *today*, neither could ever know what the other might have or might be willing to offer *tomorrow*. It is to this study of mutually beneficial, voluntary exchange between different people with different resource endowments, different tastes and potentially changing values for each of these parameters, that marketing theory addresses itself. This is the nub of the Aldersonian and Austrian positions.

In the case of the homogeneous market, a given price is the clearance mechanism. For the static heterogeneous market, differing given prices serve that function. The discrepant market, however, (which is dynamically heterogeneous) is never cleared. Full congruence is never attained. The problem is to ascertain how human beings in the discrepant marketplace act in order to maximise each other's satisfaction.

The answer lies again in differing prices. But unlike the two previous examples the prices are, not given by some *deus ex machina* but alter or are *perceived* to alter or to be about to change. Alertness to these perceived price changes results in the commencement of entrepreneurship and the market process as in Hayek's tin example (p35 above).

The entrepreneur notes, *ex ante*, that the preferences of consumers are different tomorrow from what they are today. He notes *ex ante*, that the production techniques of firms are not the same tomorrow as they are today. The Misesian entrepreneur foresees these changes in the market data. It is this foresight which is important in the discrepant market. The 'strongly motivated problem solver' of Alderson's competitive world continually faces the challenge of 'guessing right'.

The entrepreneur may make mistakes in his predictions, or he may be correct, in which case he makes respectively losses or profits. The entrepreneur must choose which prediction he believes to be correct. But he cannot simply choose to facilitate a process which equates *current* marginal valuations. Professor Shackle says: 'Decision is

115

choice amongst rival available courses of action. We can choose only what is still unactualised; we can choose only amongst imaginations and figments. Imagined actions . . . can only have imagined consequences' (Shackle, 1970, p106).

Even without changes in basic market data (consumer tastes, production possibilities and resource endowments) decisions made today generate a new series of decisions tomorrow. Today's decisions (the commencement of the market process) are made in ignorance of these market data. As the market process unfolds, this ignorance is reduced (at least in relation to current and past data) and each market participant revises his actions in the sorting process in the light of what has occurred and what he has now learned about to whom or from whom, he may wish to sell or buy. *The process is inherently competitive* since the outcome of each successive set of sorting actions is designed to be more attractive than the preceding one. That is, every individual product offering (be it in terms of price, quality, place or whatever) is being made with the awareness that all other offerings in their turn are now being made with fuller knowledge of the advantageous opportunities available. Since that is so, each individual participant knows that he cannot offer less attractive trading opportunities than his competitors. He (and they) must continually inch ahead of his (their) rivals. The competitive process of market clearing is 'analytically inseparable' from entrepreneurship.

To accomplish market clearing in a discrepant market, the entrepreneur must generally incur costs. But his net profit over costs does not arise through the surplus predicted by simple trade theory (i.e., exchanging something he values for something he values more). It comes about rather because he has been alert enough to discover sellers and buyers with such different valuations. Pure entrepreneurial profit arises from '*the discovery of something obtainable for nothing at all*' (Kirzner, 1974, p48, emphasis in original).

In rigid neo-classical orthodoxy, equilibrium already prevails in conditions of perfect competition. In a heterogeneous market, equilibrium pertains when information is adequate. In the discrepant market of Alderson and the Austrians, the market process *potentially* (but in reality never) terminates in a state of long-run equilibrium. In what Shackle called a '*Kaleidic Society*' there are always sooner or later unexpected changes which upset existing patterns, 'interspersing its moments or intervals of order, assurance and beauty with sudden disintegration and a cascade into a new pattern' (Shackle, 1972, p76).

Hence in real-life industry, where changes in technologies and consumer tastes occur, the equilibrating effort of the Misesian entrepreneur or the Aldersonian marketer is always overtaken before it has done its work. Individual markets for individual goods may, for a time, find their respective equilibria, but the macro-market system never does.

Shackle

As indicated above (p113) risk, uncertainty and ignorance are three different concepts. Loasby (1976 pp7–9) highlights this problem and shows how most writers ignore it. In the literature on management decision-taking ignorance is assumed away and subjective or objective probabilities are used in situations of risk, and techniques such as maximin and minmax regret analyses are employed in conditions of uncertainty (Luce and Raiffa, 1957).

To Austrians, however, ignorance of the future is endemic. The probability of a future state of nature cannot be calculated objectively (or even subjectively) and the various states of nature which are possible and which could result in different and uncertain outcomes are not all known to a calculating decision-taker. Only the entrepreneur can foresee (correctly or incorrectly) the future in Shackle's 'Kaleidic Society'. Only the entrepreneur can attempt to create that future (and fail or succeed). Only when the future has become the past can non-entrepreneurs assess the success of his foresight or even understand what the creative foresight was.

As Shackle said (1970, p106) entrepreneurs as acting men 'choose only what is still unactualised . . . amongst . . . figments [which] can only have imagined consequences'. How do Shackle's insights into decision-taking merge with Alderson's notion of a marketeer searching for a 'unique niche'? How do firms engage in a process of searching for and establishing a differential advantage in the Aldersonian discrepant market? There is no doubt, that even in conditions of risk, when objective probabilities are known, that the multiplicative rule of statistical probability coupled with the sheer range of alternatives makes it certain that the 'correct' choice will have an extremely small expected value. (Given the range of alternatives open not only to the firm, but to competitors, to consumers and to other environmental factors in any market.) So small that the normal gloss given by managerial economists that 'over a run of decisions' the firm will profit maximise, becomes a nonsense.

117

Even in a static heterogeneous market a 'run' must be very, if not unacceptably long. In conditions of partial ignorance any calculated outcome would be even less worthwhile since not all states of nature would be examined and the probabilities used would not even be objective. Simon's (1957) notions of 'bounded rationality' and 'satisficing' are the only neo-classical fall-back positions. Alderson (1958, p132) argued that the firm must discover its 'ecological niche': 'To succeed in competition, each firm like every blade of grass, must find a separate place to stand.'

Each decision is unique, each is an entrepreneurial act. Such acts have 'sequels', but there is a 'skein of imagined sequels', for each decision (Shackle, 1970, p106). An entrepreneur must consciously or unconsciously rank these skeins. There are two factors to be employed in such a ranking. First, the 'desiredness' of the sequel must be analysed. Second, does the sequel have a 'claim to be taken seriously'?

Shackle's expectational theory rejects probability analysis since in unique situations objective probabilities cannot be calculated and subjective ones are based on assumptions of distribution logically impossible to defend: hypothetical repetitiveness of both event *and* outcome, and, most importantly, that all possible states of nature and outcomes are included, i.e. foreseen, in the calculation of the probabilities. It is the decision-maker's inherent ignorance of all possible eventualities which is Shackle's objection to the use of probability theory, not the fact that in some cases subjective probabilities rather than objective ones are employed.

Instead, Shackle suggests (1970, chapter 5) that in the mind of the real-life entrepreneur there will only be a limited number of potential decisions and only a limited number of outcomes from each will be considered. This enables him to construct 'a non-distributional uncertainty-variable' (p112). Associated with all results will be the decision-maker's measure of belief in its occurrence. Some outcomes will be more surprising than others. Very large gains and very large potential losses may well be possible but will each have a high 'potential surprise'. Outcomes with no surprise are 'neutral' results and have a zero surprise value attached. In *Fig. 5.6* x_n indicates such a neutral outcome, whereas outcomes with higher surprise values, away from the middle of the flat bottomed basin, have higher surprise values, until they reach, Y, the level of complete incredibility. The neutral outcome zone, is that series of results which leave the decision-taker neither better nor worse off.

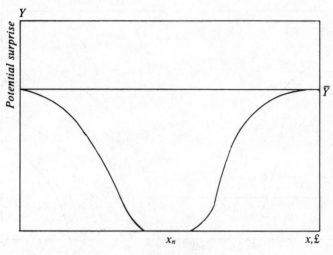

Figure 5.6

Shackle consequently argues that the bottom of the basin is of no interest to a decision-taker who wishes to improve his lot, that is, it will be irrelevant to a human actor. The actor's attention, rather, will be focused upon those outcomes which are most compelling in their foreseen gain, or most worthy of concern because of their anticipated loss.

A second function is consequently constructed to take account of the 'ascendancy, or power of a hypothesis, x, to engender the decision-maker's interest or concern' (p115). The 'ascendancy' or attention arresting power is drawn as an increasing function of x (value) and a decreasing function of Y (potential surprise). Figure 5.7 displays a map of 'equal-ascendancy' curves embodying these properties (p117) and numbered in increasing order of ascendancy. Ascendancy is thus given a zero value for all outcomes looked upon as impossible and also for all outcomes in the neutral zone.

The equal-ascendancy map of *Fig*. 5.7 and the potential surprise curve on which it is superimposed are both unique. The latter 'belongs to one specific [decision] and no other' and the former 'is a description of an individual mind' (pp119–20). The tangency points a and b are the focus outcomes, with Y_l showing the degree of potential surprise of the focus loss and Y_g that of the focus gain. X_l

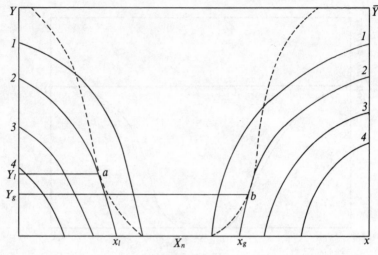

Figure 5.7

and X_g are the standardized focus outcomes which must be calculated in financial investment decisions if projects are to be compared by the decision-taker on a like-with-like basis. By doing this differing degrees of surprise between projects are eliminated and only levels of ascendancy remain to be compared.

Whether Shackle's theories can in fact assist in real-life investment decisions by businessmen (any more that Alderson's can aid marketeers) is not the issue here. The point is that Shackle, like Alderson, has moved the theory closer to meaningful reality rather than further away from it. The tractability of non-Austrian theory may be appealing but if the results are nonsense and the premises without foundation it will do little to aid understanding of human action. Shackle, however, has accomplished this and done so consistently within the Austrian praxeological tradition.

Action is only considered if it will leave man better off (hence the neutral zone of *Fig.* 5.6 is irrelevant to acting man). Only purposive action is considered. All individuals differ in tastes and values as do their perceptions of the future. Thus the ascendancy map and the potential surprise curves are unique for each action. Since action takes place through time and the future is unknown and unknowable potential surprise is a more valid concept than probabilistic measures. Since some are more alert than others in the single period what is incredible to one may not be incredible to another. In the multiperiod, the bolder, more alert, 'future creating' entrepreneur will try today to mould the potential surprise basin for any given planned course of action so that its sides are tangential to ascendancy curves giving (in his eyes) higher standardised focus gains (X_g) and lower standardised focus losses (X_l).

Thus we conclude this chapter noting how two modern writers from differing fields of managerial economics (Alderson and Shackle: from marketing and finance respectively) view decision-taking from very Austrian perspectives. Alderson's sorting process parallels Menger's and Hayek's models of movement from higher to lower order goods. Shackle, like Kirzner, does not see the future as precisely definable *ex ante*, even after a period of information search. Both see entrepreneurship rather as Marshall did: as speculative organisation. This requires both single and multiperiod alertness, concepts which enable the Schumpeterian entrepreneur to be drawn closer to the Austrian mainstream. Our discussion has enabled us to identify Marshall's 'routine superintendence' with Casson's 'trained specialist' taking 'judgemental decision'. These can be seen as tasks of modern corporate management. Neither 'superintendence' nor 'trained . . . decision taking', however, is Austrian entrepreneurship. Who then is the entrepreneur in the modern firm? It is to answering this question that the next chapter is directed.

REFERENCES

M Abramowitz, 'Resources and Output Trends in the United States since 1870', *American Economic Review*, (1956).

W Alderson, *Marketing Behaviour and Executive Action*, Irwin, (1958); *Dynamic Marketing Behaviour*, Irwin, (1965).

W J Baumol, *Economic Theory and Operations Analysis*, (3rd ed), Prentice-Hall, (1972).

K E Boulding, 'The Economics of Knowledge and the knowledge of Economics', *American Economic Review*, (1966).

M Casson, *The Entrepreneur*, Martin Robertson, (1982).

P S Florence, *The Logic of British & American Industry* (3rd ed), Routledge & Kegan Paul (1972).

I Kirzner, *Competition and Entrepreneurship*, University of Chicago Press,

(1972), *The Prime Mover of Progress*, Institute of Economic Affairs (1980); *Perception, Opportunity and Profit*, University of Chicago Press (1979); 'Uncertainty, Discovery and Human Action' in *Method, Process and Austrian Economics*, [I] Kirzner, D C Heath (eds), (1982).

A Koutsoyiannis, *Modern Microeconomics* (2nd ed), Macmillan, (1979).

S C Littlechild, *Change Rules, OK?*, University of Birmingham Press, (1977); 'Misleading Calculation of the Social Costs of Monopoly Power', *Economic Journal*, (1981).

B Loasby, *Choice, Complexity and Ignorance*, Cambridge University Press, (1976).

H Luce, and R D Raiffa, *Games and Decisions*, Wiley, (1957).

J W Markham, 'Market Structures, Business Conduct and Innovation', *American Economic Review*, (1965).

A Marshall, *Principles of Economics* (8th ed), Macmillan, (1966).

C Menger, *Principles of Economics*, New York University Press, (1981).

L von Mises, *Human Action*, Henry Regnery, (1963).

J C Narver and R Savitt, *The Marketing Economy*, Holt, Rinehart & Winston, (1971).

R R Nelson, 'Introduction' in R R Nelson, (*ed*), *The Rate and Direction of Inventive Activity*, NBER, (1962).

R R Nelson and S G Winter, 'Forces Generating and Limiting Concentration under Schumpeterian Competition', *Bell Journal of Economics*, (1978).

W D Reekie, *Industry, Prices and Markets*, Philip Allen, (1978).

W D Reekie and R Savitt, 'Market Behaviour and Entrepreneurship: A Synthesis of Alderson and Austrian Economics', *European Journal of Marketing*, (1981).

P A Samuelson, *Economics* (10th ed), McGraw Hill, (1976).

J Schmookler, 'Technological Change and Economic Theory', *American Economic Review*, (1965).

J Schumpeter, *Business Cycles*, Harrap, (1939); *Capitalism, Socialism and Democracy*, Harrap, (1942).

G L S Shackle, *Expectation, Enterprise & Profit*, George Allen & Unwin, (1970); *Epistemics and Economics*, Cambridge University Press, (1972).

H A Simon, *Models of Man*, Wiley, New York, (1957).

A Smith, *The Wealth of Nations*, (1776), Pelican edition, A Skinner (ed), 1972.

G J Stigler, 'The Economics of Information', *Journal of Political Economy*, (1961).

6 The Entrepreneur and the Firm

If the entrepreneur carries out a function of 'speculative organisation', if he does not act as a 'trained decision-taker' then who, in the modern corporation, is the entrepreneur and who are the trained decision-takers? Recent literature on the theory of the firm can help answer these questions although we will find that in doing so still wider issues are raised. This literature, sometimes Austrian in origin, sometimes not, has one thing in common: dissatisfaction with the neo-classical view of the firm as a collection of resources solely at the disposal of an identifiable wealth-maximising owner-manager. Berle and Means (1932) were the first to popularise the now familiar concept of a divorce of firm ownership from control, in that they alleged that modern corporate managers rarely (or at least decreasingly) held a legal property stake, in the form of common stock, in the companies they administered. This resulted in a plethora of theories of the firm acknowledging this apparent truism; each suggesting that managers had different motivations from owners. For example, Baumol in 1959 argued that sales maximisation was the prime managerial goal, Williamson in 1964 delineated a more broadly based managerial utility function and Marris in 1971 argued in favour of corporate growth. These views however, contrast with Austrian notions of the modern corporation. Kirzner (1972, p65) argues that if the divorce of ownership from control is such that shareholders cannot curb managerial behaviour to act exclusively in their, the shareholders' interests, then it is only because the shareholders believe, in *their* entrepreneurial judgement, that the benefits of continuing to be a shareholder in such a firm exceed the costs.

THE REASON THE FIRM EXISTS

What role then does the modern firm play in Austrian economics? To answer this question a large volume of recent literature is available, much of it stemming from the seminal (1937) paper by Ronald Coase. In this section we will also draw on the work of Williamson (1975), Jensen and Meckling (1976), Alchian and Demsetz (1972) and Fama (1980).

The fundamental question posed by Coase (1937) was to ask why on some occasions buyers and sellers transact in the market place while on others they perform similar activities in a vertically integrated firm. Coase discounts the notion that it is the presence of uncertainty which is the reason for bringing firms into existence. All production is for speculative not certain demand. All production is entrepreneurial in nature. But the entrepreneurial role is not the same as the firm's role. Entrepreneurs can be, and are, hired in the market to undertake uncertainty. For example, speculators buy stock for unpredictable resale in the commodity futures market. Again the question is left unanswered: why in some cases does entrepreneurship coincide with a firm's activities, and in others is carried on at arm's length in the market place outside the firm?

Coase concluded that firms come into existence because the costs of using the price mechanism vary. Transactions are not homogeneous. When transaction costs rise too high, when the costs of negotiating and contracting become excessive, firms come into being. A firm then is merely that area of activity within which the economies of internal organisation exceed the economies of market relationships. To bring a firm into being, to assemble resources in anticipation of a reduction in transactions costs is an entrepreneurial act. To maintain a firm in being need not be entrepreneurship.

The economies which can be obtained by replacing arms' length relationships with firms are also limited. Firms are groups or teams of people (and other resources) and groups must be co-ordinated. Co-ordination itself is not costless and may be subject to diminishing returns. Moreover, although firm or co-operative team production may result in an output which exceeds the total output which could be achieved by each team member if he operated in isolation, and although this excess may be greater than the costs of organising the firm or team, there still remains the problem of monitoring.

Alchian and Demsetz (1972) view the monitoring of effort and the rewarding of productivity as the two major problems in firm production. They argue that the inter-dependence of team production means that it is difficult to ascertain what part of total output is attributable to any one team member's efforts. Conversely, shirking may go unobserved. In individual efforts the individual reaps all the benefits of his efforts, and if he shirks he bears all the costs of shirking. But in team work, the total costs of shirking are not borne by the shirker, they are borne by the full team. Everyone admits that he is better off if no one shirks, but everyone also realises that if he alone shirks, the cost to him will be small: he can get a 'free ride' on the efforts of other team members.

More shirking will therefore occur in firms than in individual market related transactions. Shirking is cheaper in firms or teams and therefore each individual has a higher incentive to substitute leisure for productive work. The team members can get over the problem by hiring another member to monitor the productive activity of the total team. To be effective the monitor must have disciplinary powers over shirkers which can be used without disbanding the team. In short he must be able to fire a shirker. The monitor is the manager, or, more accurately in the large firm, the management group. But who monitors the monitor? How can it be ensured that managers do not shirk? The traditional legal answer is that there is a board of directors acting as shareholders' agents. We will see below, however, that the economic discussion of transaction costs, an acknowledgement that the management group is not a monolithic structure, and a willingness to perceive the possibility of competition in unwonted places can help answer this question in a far more satisfactory manner than an unreasoning acceptance of traditional legal structures *per se*.

Firstly, however, we will examine more precisely what is meant in general by the often used phrase 'transaction costs', before returning to the exact nature of how the concept aids understanding of firms and their existence.

TRANSACTION COSTS—A SIMPLE MODEL

In Chapter 5 we used Edgeworth box analysis to help understand the role of the entrepreneur, as alert arbitrageur. That simplified approach took no account (diagrammatically) of the ever changing indifference curves and production technology of real life. Nonetheless it provided some useful insights into the nature of entrepreneurial profit, but did so with only a passing mention of the phenomenon of transaction costs. The simplification can be carried even further to aid understanding of the nature of these costs. Here we use supply and demand analysis after the fashion of Alchian and Allen (1977, Ch2).

Voluntary trade occurs because people have differing marginal valuations for what they exchange. For example, in *Fig*. 6.1 Fred puts a higher marginal value on a pack of butter than does Joe (12 pints of beer against 6) at the initial endowment points of E_F and E_J (12 and 6 pints of beer respectively, and 20 packets of butter each). So mutually advantageous opportunities for trade exist.

Butter will be sold to Fred by Joe until Fred's marginal utility has declined to that of Joe's. Fred values a pack of butter at 12 pints of beer and will gladly buy an extra pack at any price below 12 pints. Joe values butter at 6 pints of beer and will gladly sell a pack for any price above 6 pints. Say Joe and Fred decide to trade at a price of 8 pints of beer, Fred will buy 4 extra packs of butter worth respectively 11, 10, 9 and 8 pints of beer to him, so increasing his stock of butter to 24 packs. Joe will sell 4 packs, reducing his stock to 16. He will receive 8 pints of beer for each pack, although they were worth respectively 6.5, 7, 7.5 and 8 pints to him.

In short, Joe will get more beer (as valued by him) than his butter is worth (to him) and Fred will get more butter (as valued by him) than his beer is worth (to him). Both will benefit by an amount equal to the shaded triangles of the diagram. Trade will have benefited both just as if there had been a magical increase in the quantity of beer.

The trading continues until both have the same marginal utilities, when no further gains from exchange are possible. Both place the same marginal value on a pack of butter. Given that the total length of the base of the diagram is the total availability of butter (40 packs) (*Fig*. 6.1) it is easy to see that originally Fred's marginal valuation of butter is higher than Joe's and trading continues until they are equal. To the left of the intersection point the gains from trade are not exhausted. To the right, both Joe and Fred are providing each other with commodities they value less than what they are acquiring.

The role of the arbitrage entrepreneur and the problem of transaction costs can be explained in terms of this discussion on trade and exchange. Consider *Fig*. 6.2 (a) in which the demand and supply curves of *Fig*. 6.1 are reproduced. Joe and Fred, it will be recalled, originally had 20 packs of butter each but each could be made better off (in his own eyes) if he traded beer for butter until Joe had 16 and

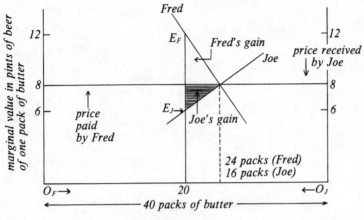

Figure 6.1

Fred had 24 packs. However, for such a trade to occur Fred and Joe must incur transaction costs. They must advertise and inform each other of their wishes. They must transport the exchanged goods and negotiate and seal the bargain.

Assume that the agreed trading price is again 8 pints of beer but that this time there are, in addition, transaction costs of 3 pints of beer per butter unit (irrespective of whether either or both individuals incur that cost). Then Fred will increase his butter holding to 22 packs, and Joe reduce his to 18. (Beer will also change hands.) Assume Fred and Joe incur the costs in a 2:1 ratio. To acquire one unit of butter Fred will willingly part (initially) with 12 pints of beer while Joe will require (initially) 6 pints. From the difference (12 – 6) of 6 pints, 3 pints of beer must be deducted in transactions costs. Thus equilibrium will only be reached in the presence of such costs when the difference in net receipts and expenditures is 3 pints of beer (in *Fig.* 6.2 (a), at a buying price of *10* and a selling price of *7* respectively). The rectangle between the two shaded areas represents the transaction costs, and less trading is done than would have been in their absence. The trade point of *Fig.* 6.1 is only worth while reaching if transaction costs are zero.

Suppose, however, that an entrepreneur believes that he can arrange for trading to be carried out more efficiently. Suppose he can do it for half the cost which Joe or Fred incur on their own. Then

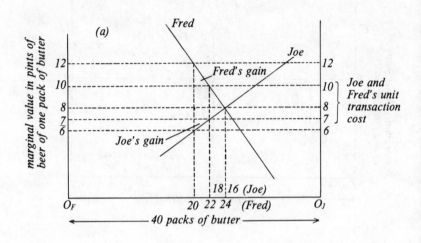

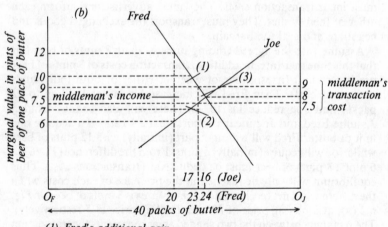

(1) Fred's additional gain
(2) Joe's additional gain
(3) further gains possible if transaction costs were zero

Figure 6.2

trading will continue until the spread between Joe's and Fred's net transaction costs prices is only 1.5, not 3 (for example, at 9 and 7.5). Both Fred and Joe are better off as a result of the arbitrageur's intervention. The entrepreneur receives an income which covers his normal costs. But again, of course, the original zero transaction cost point of 16 and 24 packs is still, and always will be, unattainable.

TRANSACTION COSTS AND THE FIRM

Williamson (1975 and 1979) complements and adds to Alchian and Demsetz's (1972) view of why firms exist. The latter emphasised the concept of team production and monitoring but did not accept contractual relationships (and hence transaction costs) as important. Indeed they said '[l]ong term contracts between employer and employee are *not* the essence of the . . . firm' (emphasis added). However, Alchian (1982, p20) now accepts that this 'assertion is incorrect' given Williamson's subsequent analyses. It is to Williamson's discussion of transaction costs, contractual relationships and hence the firm that we now turn.

Williamson's thesis commences by stressing the advantages of team activity over sequential spot contracting by market exchange. Indivisible physical resources are used for the maximum benefit of the group as a whole, and not for the benefit of a monopolistic supplier renting out time or space to individuals. Similarly, the learning-by-doing informational advantages gained by team members on the job accrue to the team as a whole. The costs of renegotiating with each worker (who is gaining ever more experience) the terms under which he will supply his (ever changing and ever scarcer) skills are eliminated or reduced. In brief, transactions costs are reduced and all reap net benefits individually as a consequence of team membership.

In addition, Williamson argues that simple, non-hierarchical teams can offer a more certain income than can individual effort coupled with insurance contracting in the market. One reason for this assertion is that *ex ante* recruitment to the team can limit membership to good risks. That is, although selection errors will be made, a policy of deliberately choosing or attempting to choose productive, well-motivated co-workers will result in the team being composed of members whose efficiency, on average, is higher than that of all individuals in the market. Insurance costs will consequently be lower in team effort than in individual effort.

Finally, Williamson takes issue with Alchian and Demsetz's 1972 view that the benefits of team production as such, namely the problem of non-separability of tasks, is why groupings of workers emerge. Alchian and Demsetz use the example of manhandling heavy loads into trucks which, to be carried out efficiently, requires two men. Such examples are alleged by Williamson to be rare or, if division of labour by individual worker is not feasible, then division of labour by small groupings certainly is. Work could pass from process to process by purchase and sale. But buffer stocks would have to be held at each interval to facilitate co-ordination and so permit the drawing up of meaningful contracts to cover the exchanges made at each stage. Thus internal organisation comes about, Williamson argues, not only because of the benefits of team production arising from non-separabilities (the original Alchian and Demsetz view) but (as with Coase, 1937) to minimise transaction costs (of haggling and of carrying relatively high inventories).

But why should peer group activity develop into hierarchical group activity? What are the specific costs which a non-hierarchical firm must meet, and what corresponding benefits accrue to a firm which removes its labour exchange activities from the extra-firm market to what Williamson calls the 'internal labour market'?

Williamson contends that non-hierarchical groups are limited by '*bounded rationality*'. In other words the human mind, even if it has an objectively rational goal, is unable to process all of the complex and voluminous information which is necessary in order to take the required decisions. The information can neither be adequately received, processed nor transmitted.

After a point the opportunity cost of wasted time by communicating everything to and from everyone for the purposes of reaching a collective decision becomes prohibitive. If scale economies of some type justify larger groupings of people then changes in organisational structure may be required. One person could, of course, be given the decision taking role in a group so that diseconomies of communication be avoided and a peer group relationship retained.

A hierarchy will almost certainly emerge, however, because of 'bounded rationality *differentials*' between the members of the group. Williamson justifies this claim on the grounds that unless leadership of the group is undemanding, or each member is equally well qualified with respect to administration, then either group productivity or group democracy must be sacrificed.

Alchian and Demsetz argued that hierarchies would emerge because of the need to monitor the performance of the group and so minimise shirking. Williamson agrees with this and gives it as the second main reason for the limitations to peer group persistence. Malingerers, he argues, can be cajoled by their fellows to work harder; if that fails, rational appeals will be made; thirdly, the group will withdraw social benefits from the offender; and, finally, the group may resort to 'overt coercion and ostracism'. When these fail the free rider or shirker may be monitored and/or awarded discriminatory wages which is 'tantamount to introducing hierarchy'.

Once a hierarchy has emerged (*vis a vis* a non-hierarchical group) what benefits accrue? Williamson argues that the resulting structure, which in effect is what is commonly called the firm, is not rigidly authoritarian but is, in itself, an internal labour market, 'an employment relation', with distinct transaction cost advantages over external labour markets.

To understand the firm as an internal labour market (and so an entity which is not just a 'black box' but one to which economic or market analysis is applicable) it is necessary also to realise that, although property rights in specific tasks are relatively weak, '*job idiosyncracy*' exists. Williamson argues that 'job idiosyncracy' or non-homogeneity occurs because workers acquire 'job specific skills and related task-specific knowledge' comparable to the knowledge of Hayek's 'man-on-the-spot'.

Thus workers progressively obtain more and more knowledge of the kind Hayek termed 'particular circumstances of time and place'. This results in asymmetry either in the information held by members of a firm and/or in the costs of acquiring that information. (Williamson defines this phenomenon as '*information impactedness*'.) But information impactedness is precisely the reason why normal market transactions occur. Entrepreneurs spot opportunities for mutually beneficial exchange between buyers and sellers, help initiate a suitable transaction and so move the market towards equilibrium.

In analogous manner, *within* the firm, the firm itself is moved towards its objective (or equilibrium) as members enter into mutually beneficial trades or contracts. Such exchanges occur, even in a hierarchical situation, because the parties to the exchange place

131

different marginal valuations on the commodities (for simplicity, say labour and cash) they are trading. The differing marginal valuations arise due to information impactedness. The superior has unique information relating to the income the firm can obtain from a given set of productive inputs. The subordinate has unique know-how, arising from experience, relating to the task he will be called upon to perform. This makes it easier (i.e. cheaper) for him to perform that task at the margin and so makes it easier for him to compete against a willing but inexperienced subordinate (for example, an outsider) who would have to incur training and learning costs.

What kind of contractual relationship then is the most efficient? Williamson examines five. Only one is regarded as sufficiently flexible to permit adaptation to changing internal and external market circumstances. Only that one is also able to overcome the problems of opportunism (for example shirking), peer group organisation, and task idiosyncracy. That one is the internal labour market. We will initially survey the demerits of the other four.

First, a contract could be made now with a subordinate (or group of subordinates) to perform a specific task in the future. This, however, is impractical (i.e. too costly to implement) in complex and uncertain business environments and can be dismissed as of little practical interest. A second alternative is to draw the contract up in probabilistic or contingent terms to account for such uncertainties. An agreed wage would be paid now in return for future services which would depend on circumstances. Williamson argues that business life is too complex to write such employment contracts feasibly or cheaply *ex ante*. Bounded rationality would prohibit it. Even if it were feasible to write the contracts at reasonable expense, Williamson then argues that there would be problems of comprehensibility which would impede agreement. At least one party to the contract (probably the worker) would not fully understand the ramifications of the complex agreement to which he is being asked to accede. Information impactedness would be an obstacle. *Ex post*, the contract would face enormous enforcement problems. Opportunism could result in shirking. Information impactedness could result in disputes over which contingent state of the world had, in fact, come to pass. And resort to arbitration would not, by definition, reduce the information impactedness problem. The arbitrator himself would face the problem as to how much of the apparent or claimed knowledge asymmetry regarding the state of the world was real and how much was due to opportunism (lack of candour or honesty in drawing up or executing the transaction).

The third alternative is sequential contracting: i.e. a series of short-term contracts in the spot market. This concept permits continuous adaptation of the contract to changing circumstances and so overcomes the problems of uncertainty. Bounded rationality and information impactedness pose much less severe problems since no attempt is made to detail all contingencies in advance and so, *ex post*, there need be no dispute over which state of the world had come to pass. This was the original Alchian and Demsetz (1972) view of the firm. Williamson, however, denies that sequential spot contracting can be applied to the situation of the firm because of unacceptably high transaction costs. It is inefficient in that there is scope for opportunistic behaviour due to task idiosyncracy. This 'effectively destroys parity (with outsiders) at the contract renewal interval. Incumbents who enjoy non-trivial advantages over similarly qualified but inexperienced bidders are well-situated to demand some fraction of the cost savings which their idiosyncratic experience has generated.' Such problems of opportunism can only be overcome if workers are either asked to bid for employment contracts by offering lump sums to employers reflecting the present value of the monopoly gains which will accrue to them due to their idiosyncratic experience (but this reintroduces issues of bounded rationality and information impactedness); or if workers promise not to behave opportunistically when contracts come up for renegotiation, which assumes they will behave irrationally; or if workers submit to authoritarian monitoring.

Authority is the fourth form of contractual relationship. Simon (1957) suggests an authoritarian agreement exists if a worker is willing to accept a boss's authority in exchange for a stated wage. This type of agreement will be preferred to an extra-firm 'sales contract' provided that a deterministic (wholly certain) sales contract cannot be drawn up and that the area of uncertainty which does remain (what the worker will, in fact, be asked to do) will not prove unattractive to the worker. It will be advantageous to the boss to draw up such a contract if he wishes to postpone the precise selection of the worker's task until some time after the contract is made. Simon's authority contract is simply one in which the parties 'agree to tell and be told'. But, Williamson argues, 'the terms are rigged from the outset'. The 'sales contract' with which Simon compares his authority relation is merely our first contractual (and flexible) alternative. Our second and third possibilities (a contingent sales contract and a series of sequential spot contracts) both offered the advantages of flexibility in response to changing circumstances. Does the authority relation, then, offer anything in terms of efficiency? It is less costly than the contingent sales contract in that it does not impose the bounded rationality problem and so high transaction costs of generating knowledge of all alternative outcomes in advance. It is superior to the spot contracting mode in that transaction costs are lowered due to the decrease in frequency with which contracts are negotiated. Nevertheless, all of the problems of task idiosyncracy which were present in spot contracting remain to be faced. For example, how are terms of employment to be adjusted over time as circumstances change? How are the problems of disputes due to either opportunism or information impactedness to be resolved? With job idiosyncracy firms will either have to bear the high costs of continuous labour turnover or the high costs of meeting the demands of idiosyncratic workers with monopoly bargaining power.

The fifth possibility, the internal labour market is, if not optimal in terms of minimising transactions costs between firms and employees, possibly the closest approach to optimality yet suggested. In particular, it overcomes the problems posed by task idiosyncracies. The essence of the employment relation or the internal labour market is that the individual contract is replaced by the collective bargain. This results, to cite Williamson, (1975, p74) in a 'fundamental transformation . . . where wage rates are attached mainly to jobs rather than to workers'. The incentive to behave opportunistically which individual workers would have in individual contracting (due to their peculiar experience) is thus greatly reduced. The collective agreement also overcomes problems of uncertainty by being written in general terms which makes it 'an instrument of government as well as exchange'.

All individuals who collectively accede to the contract presumably do so because they feel it is to their individual net advantage. Each has an area within which he is indifferent as to what instruction he may receive from those to whom he has granted authority or powers of government. But any one individual whose area of indifference is opportunistically distinct from those of the rest of the group will not, provided the distinction is small, reject authority. Should he do so he would pose a threat to the benefits of all the other individuals who gain from the agreement. Thus group pressures would be exerted against such opportunistic behaviour and the authority relationship embodied in the contract be reinforced from below.

Bounded rationality is attenuated by writing the contract in non-precise terms. Information impactedness, *ex post*, or disagreements in contractual interpretation resulting in disputes, are provided for by writing into the contract, *ex ante*, details of dispute-settling mechanisms. This allows the day-to-day running of the firm to be pursued while the grievance is tackled by the arbitration apparatus devised by the parties to the contract. Since this apparatus may be composed of some sort of elected group (such as a union committee) representing the workers as a whole, it will be more concerned with the interests of the total labour force. Thus, again, opportunistic behaviour due to task idiosyncracy is curbed.

But the acceptance of the employment relation does not ensure that the firm receives 'consummate' as opposed to 'perfunctory' co-operation from its labour force. The former is described by Williamson as an 'affirmative job attitude' including the 'use of judgement, filling gaps, and taking initiative in an instrumental way'. The latter, by contrast 'involves job performance of a minimally acceptable sort—where minimally acceptable means that incumbents who have idiosyncratic advantages, 'need merely to maintain a slight margin over the best available inexperienced candidate'.

Consummate co-operation could be obtained by awarding in-dividual incentive payments of a sequential spot contract kind but this is precluded in the collective bargains of internal labour markets. Williamson argues instead that the advantages of internal labour markets can be maintained, but consummate co-operation also obtained, if, as part of the internal incentive system, higher level positions are generally filled by internal promotions. If such practices are followed by most firms the internal labour market is strengthened.

Other implications follow. The firm can risk avert by only employing newcomers at low levels in the hierarchy. This protects the firm against opportunistic job applicants who might represent themselves as more productive than they otherwise are. Promotion will only follow as experience warrants it. Restricting 'ports of entry' to low level jobs reflects the advantages of the internal market over the external labour market in other ways as well. Any lateral transfer which could occur between firms at higher levels because an employee is motivated to move due to a (correct) denial of promotion in his original firm is less likely. Interim information impactedness might otherwise have resulted in such a transfer taking place. The new employer would not have had the advantage of the old employer's hierarchy to provide him with information relating to the defects of the new entrant. Moreover, opportunism by the old employer could have resulted in problems of veracity regarding the quality of the new entrant. The old employer might have been only too happy to be rid of the employee (who might have reached his existing level in the old firm as a consequence of a rating error in the first place).

In short, intra-firm labour markets, hierarchies, have informational advantages over extra-firm labour markets. They are less subject to bounded rationality, information impactedness, and to opportunistic behaviour. They are better than perfunctory cooperation as a consequence of their hierarchical structure. And a monitor, indeed a hierarchy of monitors, in the Alchian and Demsetz sense, is still required.

THE DIVORCE OF OWNERSHIP FROM CONTROL: A CHALLENGE TO AUSTRIANISM?

We have now established that the divorce of ownership from control does not mean that the firm needs to be viewed as a 'black box'. The extent of the 'divorce' is, of course, an empirical question. But that it exists, even if the degree to which it exists is not a subject for consensus, is not in doubt. However, even if we can now apply economic analysis *within* the firm as well as between firms does this necessarily make any impact on the claim that managers can pursue objectives fundamentally different from those of wealth-maximising shareholders?

The answer is no. Part of the apparent difficulty in seeing this is in the taxonomy of 'manager', 'worker' and 'shareholder'. The very words inculcate an image of antagonists rather than complementary team members. The Alchian and Demsetz notion of a team overcomes the problem. The firm is merely a team which exists (or, set of contractual agreements negotiated) for the benefit of all team members. Some are wealthier than others. Some are risk preferrers. Others are more risk averse. Some have talents of monitoring and selection. Others have a comparative advantage in energy, knowledge and skills as producers. Provided property rights exist in these

136

interpersonal differences they can be freely exchanged. Each individual will still care only for his own personal benefit when negotiating the exchange (such is the restricted thesis of the divorce of ownership from control) but each will only enter into the contractual agreement known as a firm if each believes he will be better off thereby. The firm is simply another example of mutually beneficial exchange.

There is nothing authoritarian, dictatorial or exploitative in the relationship. Employees order employers to pay them amounts specified in the hiring contract just as much as employers order employees to abide by the terms of the contract. The team itself, however, is hired and fired with abandon in the (spot) market place by consumers. There are two types of team member who gain or suffer from satisfying or failing to satisfy consumers. One is the *fixed reward claimant* and the other is the *residual claimant* (or shareholder).

Fixed reward claimants are shielded in the short run from the exigencies of demand by the terms of their contract. They must be paid whether the residual claim is large or negative. Residual claimants do not have this cushion. In the long run, claimants with fixed payment contracts can move to other teams to preserve their contractual claims.

But does the modern firm permit more or less opportunism than alternative forms of organisation? Williamson (1979) argued that cost economising is of the essence in commercial transactions. Costs are of two kinds: production expenses and transaction costs. In situations where transaction costs are negligible buying-in rather than making is optimal since scale economies can be fully exploited. When transaction costs are higher, or the potential for savings in production expenses is less then the balance alters. Economising on transaction costs 'essentially reduces to economising on bounded rationality while simultaneously safeguarding the transactions . . . against the hazards of opportunism' (Williamson, 1979, p246). Thus for recurrent transactions a make decision is more likely than a buy-in decision since bounded-rationality costs are minimised by saving the expense of continuously rewriting contracts. The more idiosyncratic or seller:customer-specific is the traded good the more complex must the contract be and so the greater is the potential attenuation of bounded rationality. On the other hand, Williamson points out that monitoring costs then rise as the contractor has now to ensure contract execution and guard against opportunism. Such monitoring (transaction) costs begin to exceed the benefits of economising on bounded rationality (transaction costs) the less frequent is the execution of the relationship between the two parties. This is because of inadequate monitoring skills. Thus after a point, as a recurrent transaction becomes less frequent one aspect of transaction costs outweighs the other and a buy decision becomes more likely.

Williamson (1979) uses the phrase *'governance structures'* (p247) to distinguish between *market transactions, neo-classical contracting* (where formal legal contracts are involved and a third party, the civil law, is used to aid in both contract construction and execution) and *relational contracting*. Relational contracting is further subdivided into *unified governance* (the firm) and *bilateral governance* where two equal but independent partners buy and sell from each other. Williamson then matched commercial transaction types with governance structures as in Table 6.1. The dotted lines simply indicate definitional and illustrative imprecision in the analysis. The firm is only unambiguously present as the most efficient governance structure in one of the six cells.

This analysis, however, only helps explain why the firm may be the most efficient structure in certain circumstances. We still have not definitely answered the question whether it has become more or less so since the alleged divorce of ownership from control came to the attention of some writers.

The reasons the corporate team, including its monitors, continues to work in the interests of residual claimants or owners, are twofold. First, there is the presence of an active internal (and external) labour market for monitors (or managers). Second there is the market in corporate control.

Management is not a monolith but rather a group of self-interested persons seeking to displace others. Managers are in competition with fellow incumbents and outside challengers. As Fama (1980, pp291–4) points out, managers rent their wealth, or human capital, to the team and the 'rental rates . . . signalled by the management labour market . . . depend on the success or failure of the firm'. How do the pressures work?

Managers are 'sorted and compensated' (Fama, p292) according to performance. Since the firm is always in the market for new managers it must be able to explain to potential recruits how they will be rewarded. If the reward system is not responsive to performance the

Characteristic of Traded Good

Purchase Frequency	Non-Specific	Mixed	Idiosyncratic
Occasional	Standard Equipment MARKET or CLASSICAL CONTRACT	Customised Equipment NEO-CLASSICAL CONTRACT	Plant Construction NEO-CLASSICAL CONTRACT
Recurrent	Standard Material MARKET or CLASSICAL CONTRACT	Customised Material BILATERAL	Site-Specific Transfer of a Higher Order Good for Conversion to a Lower Order UNIFIED
		RELATIONAL CONTRACT	

Table 6.1

Source: Williamson, 1979.

firm will not be able to either recruit or retain the best managers. Conversely, but by the same argument, managers, especially top managers, have a stake in the firm's performance since the external market uses that as a means of determining his opportunity wage. In the internal management market monitoring is part of a manager's role. Part of his talent is the ability to monitor lower levels of management, gauge their performance and reward them accordingly. And, as Fama (p293) points out, this monitoring process operates from lowest levels upwards as well. 'Lower managers perceive that they can gain by stepping over shirking or less competent [seniors] . . . [while] in the nexus of contracts . . . each manager is concerned with the performance of managers above and below him since his marginal product is likely to be a positive function of theirs.'

Furthermore, given 'competition among the top managers . . . to be the boss of bosses' (Fama, p293) they are perhaps 'the best ones to control the board of directors'. Their specialised knowledge plus their market determined opportunity wages may render them 'the most informed and responsive critics of the firm's performance'.

The chances of collusion by such senior managers to expropriate the wealth of shareholders by not pursuing wealth-maximising goals is minimised by the managerial market mechanism already described and by the market in corporate control. This latter is the market in which another group of specialists in the team operate. These are the specialists who are willing to accept risk and engage in residual claim contracts with the remainder of the team. It is the shareholder's willingness to bear the costs and benefits of the changing value of the firm which makes him the owner of the firm. Alchian (1982, p25) points out that there are four separable tasks in exercising property rights: (a) selecting resource use, (b) monitoring input performance, (c) revising contracts or replacing inputs, and (d) bearing the value changes of resources. 'The first three can be delegated to fiduciary agents acting as specialists, but the fourth cannot'. (This is not to deny the existence for some commodities of future markets where owners can hedge to minimise risk of loss. But the operation and successful outcome of such hedging activity is the direct consequence of the resource owner bearing a value loss on one bundle of resources and an offsetting value gain on another. Future markets permit this type of activity to 'reduce or control risk' but it is still the resource owner who bears the value changes. Similarly, the resource owner may delegate the monitoring task to a specialist to 'reduce or control risk' but he still bears the value change of the resource consequential to the delegation.)

The market in corporate control was most eloquently described by Manne in 1965. Like the managerial market this market also ensures that the divorce of ownership from control is more apparent than real. Directors and managers cannot long depart from the wealth-maximisation objectives of shareholders or they will be displaced by the take-over mechanism (the corporate control market). Information on management performance is disclosed by the price of the firm's shares. The stock market thus provides not only price signals about where to 'invest' and disinvest financial resources but it also provides information about management which can be used to allocate rewards and penalties. A poorly managed firm will suffer from a declining share price. Stockholders will sell to higher bidders who perceive that replacing the management team will improve the firm's performance and so share price. Hence poor managers will either be removed or stimulated to improve their performance by the operation of the stock market. 'Without a stock market, information about performance of managers would be more difficult to obtain' (Alchian, 1982, p27) and the advantages of specialisation within the team (risk-bearing and monitoring respectively) could then appear to be outweighed by the costs of opportunism resulting from delegation. So task specialisation and resulting efficiency is encouraged by the presence of a stock market, and those who bewail the 'divorce of ownership from control' have failed to see that what the modern joint stock company permits is a marriage of productive convenience between internal labour markets and entrepreneurship. It is not a device which results in an autonomous Galbraithian technocracy responsible to no one but itself.

ENTREPRENEURSHIP AGAIN

Marriage partners, however, as the Bible tell us 'are no more twain, but are one flesh'. In analytic or legalistic terms it may in many situations be impossible to distinguish husband from wife. So, analogously, in the marriage of convenience which is the modern corporation it may be impossible to ascertain who the entrepreneur is.

Mises (1966, pp303–11) argues that the entrepreneurial function can exist at all levels in the hierarchical firm, but warns that it is a serious error to confuse the entrepreneur with any particular category in the hierarchy. 'The manager is a junior partner of the entrepreneur . . . [whose] own financial interests force him to attend to the best of his abilities to the entrepreneurial functions which are assigned to him within a limited and precisely determined sphere of action.' In a firm which is subject to what Mises terms 'profit management', entrepreneurship can be delegated. Profit centres can be set up within a business and the entrepreneur can allocate tasks to each and appraise each centre according to the profits it contributes to the total business. Each division can be regarded as an autonomous business buying and selling to other divisions and to the outside market. Thus the entrepreneur can assign to each section's management a great deal of independence. Within circumscribed limits divisional managers need merely to be told to make as much profit as possible:

Every manager and sub-manager is responsible for the working of his section or sub-section . . . If he incurs losses, he will be replaced . . . If he succeeds in making profits his income will be increased or at least he will not be in danger of losing it . . . His task is not like that of the technician, to perform a definite piece of work according to a definite precept. It is to adjust—within the limited scope left to his discretion—the operation of his section to the state of the market.

Thus employees in a firm at any level in the hierarchy can exercise an entrepreneurial role. The area within which that role can be carried out increases the more authority the employee has. But the manager, no matter how high, can never be the entrepreneur since he 'cannot be made answerable for the losses incurred'. In the final analysis, Mises argues, the entrepreneur is the owner. He alone determines the grand strategy of the business. He may call on managerial advice but the decisions are his. Decisions as to 'what lines of business to employ capital [in] and how much capital to employ . . . [decisions as to] expansion and contraction of the size of the total business, and its main sections . . . [decisions as to its] financial structure' fall upon the entrepreneur alone.

The mechanism used to ensure this is the market for corporate control, the stock market. The prices of stocks and shares 'are the means applied by the capitalists for the supreme control of the flow of capital . . . [this] decides how much capital is available for the conduct of each corporation's business; it creates a state of affairs to which the managers must adjust their operations in detail'.

Not only is this a positivist description of the industrial firm it is also, Mises argues, normatively desirable:

Society can freely leave the care for the best possible employment of capital goods to their owners. In embarking upon definite projects these owners expose their own property, wealth and social position. They are even more interested in . . . success . . . than is society as a whole. For society as a whole the squandering of capital invested in a definite project means only the loss of a small part of its total funds; for the owner it means much more . . . But if a manager is given a completely free hand, things are different. He speculates in risking other people's money. He sees the prospects of an uncertain enterprise from another angle than that of the man who is answerable for the losses . . . he becomes foolhardy because he does not share in the losses too.

Thus, the entrepreneurial function can be partially delegated as Alchian suggested, to a fiduciary agent or manager. In the ultimate, however, the entrepreneur himself remains the owner of the property rights whose value can rise or fall. To ensure that he retains these property rights the market in corporate control must be subject to effective competition. So too must the internal management market. These two conditions hold most obviously when there is a stock market with a diffusion (or potential diffusion) of ownership. And secondly, when the transaction costs of hiring managers by a firm (to Williamson, a 'unified, relational contract') are less than those of other governance structures. By this analysis, if society is to be optimally served by the entrepreneurial function, the divorce of ownership from control must be a fiction. The reality should be a marriage of convenience between the internal management and labour markets and the entrepreneur.

CONCLUSION

At first glance the above pages have given two mutually exclusive answers to our attempt to identify the entrepreneur. The first is that he is everywhere. This is simply a restatement of the general principle of human action that man acts in anticipation of gain. Employees, managers and shareholders were all seen to behave entrepreneurially. The second answer is that the entrepreneur is restricted to the

143

shareholder, in which case much of the above discussion is redundant.

The paradox is resolved and the conflict removed if we bear in mind that anticipated gain is not synonymous with anticipated corporate profits. The latter is only a sub-set of the former. Everyone acts for anticipated gain but only shareholders act unambiguously to acquire corporate profits. The role of internal labour markets and the market in corporate control is simply that of ensuring that the conflict of interest between non-shareholder entrepreneurs and shareholder-entrepreneurs is minimised. If this is achieved then delegation of the shareholder-entrepreneur's function can be achieved successfully without removing from him what Knight (1921, p271) identified as the essential roles of control and responsibility.

As a digression it is worth pointing out that while Austrians agree with Knight on this last point they do not accept his explanation of profits as an *ex post* residual reward for bearing uncertainty. As Kirzner (1972, p83) emphasises, entrepreneurs act as a consequence of their alertness, *ex ante*, and they envisage (prior to acting) only one possibility, positive profits. To Austrians alertness to entrepreneurial profit results in action. To Knight the bearing of uncertainty in an action results, possibly, in profits.

The above discussion has also highlighted, *inter alia*, that the terms 'entrepreneur' and 'firm' are not synonymous. Although traditional neo-classical text books often use the words interchangably they are misleading (as the proponents of the notion of the concept of the divorce of ownership from control have pointed out, albeit from a different stance from the above arguments). As McNulty (1968) said, in a *cri de coeur*, '. . . although economic activity encompasses both production [in the firm] and exchange [in the market], the concept of competition has been generally associated only with the latter'. Competition within the firm, although written about by Mises, has only become overt in the literature since Alchian, Demsetz, Manne and Williamson have emphasised the nature of the firm, transaction costs, property rights and the markets in corporate control and in management. The entrepreneur is he who brings together resources into an entity known as 'the firm'. He sells the output of those resources using the firm as his production instrument. The firm is instigated by the entrepreneur. The original entrepreneur may die or be replaced, as may the firm. But entrepreneurial elements within the firm, as a team, can arise and prevent this. They themselves can earn rewards of a supranormal level either as workers, managers, or shareholders. Given the workings of the markets in corporate control and in management, shareholders as the ultimate capitalists cannot long be deprived of such entrepreneurial rewards. And if they are so deprived it is because, in their own entrepreneurial view, it is less costly continuing to employ the other team members than to carry out the latters' functions themselves.

This notion that the entrepreneurial function can exist at any level in the hierarchical firm is emphasised by Mises when he contrasts 'profit management' with 'bureaucratic management'. The internal management market operates in different ways for these two types of management, and the role of entrepreneurship varies. It is to this difference and to other aspects of Austrian economics which impinge upon bureaucracy, real or apparent, towards which the next chapter is directed.

REFERENCES

A Alchian and W R Allen, *Exchange and Production; Competition, Coordination and Control*, 2nd edition, Wadsworth, (1979).

A Alchian, 'Property Rights, Specialisation and the Firm', J F Weston and M E Granfield (eds), *Corporate Enterprise in A New Environment*, KCG Productions, (1982).

A Alchian and H Demsetz, 'Production Information Costs and Economic Organisation', *American Economic Review*, (1972).

W J Baumol, *Business Behaviour, Value and Growth*, Macmillan, New York, (1959).

A A Berle and G C Means, *The Modern Corporation and Private Property*, Macmillan, New York, (1972).

R H Coase, 'The Nature of the Firm', *Economica*, (1932).

E F Fama, 'Agency Problems and the Theory of the Firm', *Journal of Political Economy*, (1980).

M C Jensen and W H Meckling, 'Theory of the Firm, Management Behaviour, Agency Costs and Ownership Structure', *Journal of Financial Economics*, (1976).

I Kirzner, *Competition and Entrepreneurship*, University of Chicago Press, (1972).

I Knight, *Risk, Uncertainty and Profit*, Houghton, Mifflin, (1921).

R Marks, R Marris and A Wood (eds.), *The Corporate Economy*, Macmillan, London, (1971).

L. von Mises, *Human Action*, Henry Regnery, 1966.

P J McNulty, 'Economic Theory and the Meaning of Competition', *Quarterly Journal of Economics*.
H A Simon, *Models of Man*, Wiley, (1957).
O E Williamson, *The Economics of Discretionary Behaviour*, Prentice Hall, (1964), *Markets and Hierarchics*. Free Press, (1975); 'Transaction Cost Economics: The Governance of Contractual Relations', *Journal of Law and Economics*, (1979).

7 Politics, Bureaucracy and Commercialism

In this chapter we examine how Austrian theory can be applied, not only to unwonted areas such as within the firm (as opposed to between firms) as was illustrated in the previous chapter but also to unexpected, non-commercial areas in the political scene. Not all Austrian writers are agreed on the role of government. That debate does not concern us here. The reason why we have a government (and a bureaucracy to implement its laws) lies in the presence of 'externalities'. David Hume (1960, p538) explained this concept using the illustration of a meadow which could be profitably drained. If one man owned the meadow he would drain it, and capture the profit. (This assumed he was alert to the possibility.) Hume argued if there were two common owners of the meadow, they would in turn agree on the division of the cost of and profit from draining the meadow. However, if there were 20 people whose property the meadow straddled agreement to drain would still be sensible for all in aggregate but very difficult to arrive at in practice. Each is aware that his abstention will only slightly reduce the resources available for drainage, but that he will still get his share of the benefits at no cost if he so abstains. Consequential hard bargaining might well leave the meadow undrained. Hume thus recommended the use of government for such circumstances. His view was *not* based on the premise that a collectively coerced outcome is necessarily superior to a privately negotiated one, but that the alternative to the imposed solution is no outcome at all.

And these, of course, are the key issues. When government provides a good the provision is of an all or nothing nature, the good is generally homogeneous and there are transaction costs of using a bureaucracy. This does not imply that the good should not be provided, or that there should be variations in the nature of supply, or that there are not transaction costs in market provision. It simply means that the two forms of institution should be compared to find

147

which more truly meets consumer requirements for the good in question. We will now examine these points in more detail.

PUBLIC GOODS AND EXTERNALITIES

To this point we have restricted our discussion solely to private goods (i.e. goods which are scarce, or (what is the same thing) economic goods). When a good does not suffer from reduced availability due to consumption it is called a *public good*. As consumers increase in number the same given amount is available. National defence is a classic example; so too is a television broadcast or a football game. In addition, people often cannot be excluded from the benefits provided by the good. Thus if my house is saved (or not saved) from nuclear extinction by the effectiveness (or ineffectiveness) of defence forces the same result will also occur for my next-door neighbours. However, it becomes ever more possible to exclude outsiders as human ingenuity grows. In the simple case of the football game, the match is a public good until the point when someone decides to erect enclosures and stadia with only a few gates at which would-be spectators must pay. Similarly, cable-transmitted television (as opposed to wireless transmission) not only permits a wider choice of programmes but provides access to those programmes only if the viewer pays for the rental of the cable, or alternatively has a meter built into the set which registers the amount owing by the viewer to the broadcast company.

Another assumption made so far is that whenever a trade occurs all the costs and benefits from the exchange accrue only to the transactors. This need not be the case. For example, one consumer may heat his house with oil and pay the fuel company for the oil consumed. But the cost of his heating may not be fully reflected in his fuel bill if the oil refinery produced a large amount of air pollution.

In effect, part of the cost of heating the consumer's house is being borne by others. They are subsidising him. They may not use oil-fired heating themselves but they are involuntarily consuming dirty air. This is an external cost or *negative externality* (since it is external to the transaction which resulted in it). External benefits or *positive externalities* arise if, for example, a house-holder goes to his local garden nursery, purchases flowering shrubs for his garden, and makes his own property pleasant and appealing to look at.

Externalities only occur if property rights do not exist. When private property rights are well defined and easily enforced there is no cause for concern about externalities. We will examine first this situation, and second the problems of government policy when externalities persist.

The former proposition was first advanced by Ronald Coase (1961) and is now known as the *Coase theorem*. The theorem states that efficiency will always be realised in the absence of transaction costs no matter how property rights are assigned. Consider an example used by Coase himself. There is a strip of unfenced, unowned land between the property of a grain farmer and a cattle farmer. The grain farmer would like to plant grain but the cattle would inevitably damage it in whole or in part, so he does not cultivate the land. This may or may not be socially optimal. If society values grain at the margin more highly than cattle it is certainly not optimal, since the grain farmer cannot or will not use the land, while the cattle farmer can graze more cattle at zero grazing cost (zero cost to himself: he gains an external benefit). Nevertheless society would prefer the land to be used for grain.

Now assume that we do not know which use is more efficient from society's point of view. But assume the grain farmer takes a chance that he can plant grain and get a profit from the sale of at least some undamaged portion of it. He also decides to sue the cattle farmer for damages to his crop. The law court will, of course, find it very difficult to decide whether or not to aware damages. Both farmers had equal rights (i.e. no rights, or only squatter's rights) to the land. The judge must make a value judgement. Let us assume he decides to award full private ownership of the land to one party or the other.

The important factor emerging from the Coase theorem is that once this award is made, irrespective of the direction of the judgement (in favour of the grain or the cattle farmer), the land will now be put to its most efficient, most socially highly valued use. Table 7.1 explains why, showing the outcome if the judgement is (a) in favour of the cattle farmer and (b) in favour of the grain farmer. It also considers the increased profits of each farmer if he secures legal access to the land relative to his profits if he had no such access.

Thus the Coase theorem is proved, and efficiency is realised no matter to whom the land is assigned by the legal authorities (albeit the wealth of the farmer to whom the land was awarded will increase). However, there are always transaction costs in real life. The Coase theorem, boldly stated, assumes them away. Rental agreements must be entered into between the farmers. Negotiation expenses must be incurred, most obviously, in this example, fencing costs are necessary to keep the cattle off the grain. In this example, if transaction costs (on a yearly basis) amount to £400 or more then, even if situation (a) 2 occurs, cattle will be farmed. This is because the profits on farming grain less the transaction costs will be below £600, leaving no positive net profits with which to pay a rental to the cattle farmer. (Which party actually incurs the cost of fencing and other transaction

Property rights awarded to the farmer of	
(a) Cattle	(b) Grain

1 *Additional profits per annum from use of the land*

Cattle farmer £1000: the cattle farmer will farm cattle on the land and earn £1000 extra profit.	Grain farmer £600: the cattle farmer will farm cattle on the land, earn £1000, but pay a rental to the grain farmer which must be above £600 (or grain will be farmed) and below £1000 (or it will be unprofitable to graze cattle).

2 *Additional profits*

Cattle £600: the grain farmer will grow crops, paying the cattle farmer a rent of over £600 but under £1000.	Grain £1000: the grain farmer will use the land, the profit of £1000 indicating that this is its most socially highly valued use.

Table 7:1

expenses is not really relevant, it is the amount which matters.) Once the property rights are assigned the grain farmer will always be able to claim damages from the cattle farmer if the land is assigned to him and he uses it for grain growing and not rental. Thus the cattle (grain) farmer will be motivated to fence in (out) the cattle to avoid paying for (losing) any grain. What it will affect obviously, will be the upper limit to the rental the grain farmer is willing and able to pay.

The first main lesson from the Coase theorem is that externalities can often be 'internalised' if property rights can be established and means of charging devised. Thus public goods may not be so common as supposed. The classic lighthouse example given by Paul Samuelson (1976, p49) is not necessarily a public good. In America it is provided by government. But in Britain, Trinity House in England and the Commissioners for Northern Lights in Scotland, plus other bodies, built substantial numbers of lighthouses in the nineteenth century, collecting tolls from ships when they entered the harbour.

Another textbook example is that of beekeepers whose bees receive nectar free of charge from fruit tree owners (an external benefit) but provide cross-pollination services without charge (a negative externality to the beekeeper). Steven Cheung (1978) dismissed this example. He discovered that in California there were three groups of fruit orchards: those which provided nectar with a high honey potential; those with a moderate honey potential and those which provided little or no honey potential. All, however, required pollination and cross-fertilisation by bees and other insects. Cheung found a well-developed market, contrary to the textbook writers. Orchard owners with fruit trees of the first type charged the apiary owners a site rental to leave their hives in the orchard. Those of the third type paid apiary owners to leave their hives in the orchards during the relevant seasons. The middle grouping came to more or less no-charge agreements because the respective alleged externalities cancelled out.

The second lesson from the Coase theorem is that externalities can still occur, and if property rights cannot be established or transaction costs minimised then market failure will arise. How can it be minimised? What does the demand curve look like for a public good? Unlike the market demand curve for a private good (obtained by adding each individual's demand curve horizontally), to obtain the market demand curve for a public good the addition is vertical. For private goods if one extra unit was made available only one individual could consume it (so we move along the Q axis of the demand diagram) and this consumer would value the good at its market price (so we remain at the same position on the P axis). With public goods, however, everyone benefits if one extra unit is provided, so the value of that unit is the sum of the values all consumers place on it. To reflect this we must move up the P axis.

With this tool-kit we can now look at some of the problems of public good provision. What is the optimal provision of the public good? Figure 7.1 shows a three-citizen community where the demand curves D_1, D_2 and D_3 represent their relevant marginal valuation curves. Curve D is equal to $D_1 + D_2 + D_3$ added vertically at any given Q. MC is the marginal cost of providing the good. At output Q' social marginal benefits received equal social marginal costs; Q' is consequently the optimal output.

But here we encounter the next difficulty. Although output Q' is socially optimal, only one individual values the good sufficiently highly to pay a price for the first few units which will cover the

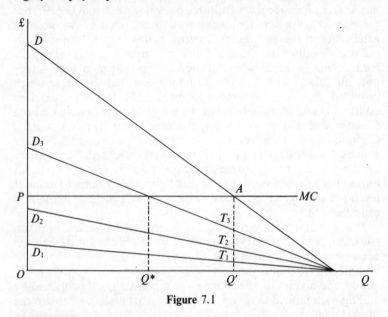

Figure 7.1

marginal cost. This is individual 3. He will buy up to Q^* and then cease purchasing. In short, with public goods, everyone wants them, but few, and sometimes none, are prepared to pay for them.

In addition, if individual 3 does pay for Q^* units then the other two members of the community are *free-riding* at his expense. They are obtaining the benefits without incurring any costs. All three members of society would prefer Q' units, which would increase their net benefits to equal the area DPA, the maximum net benefit they can collectively obtain.

With three individuals a collective agreement could possibly be hammered out to ensure that Q' units were produced. With a large nation the solution to the problem is usually obtained by handing the task over to government who will fund the provision through taxation. Again *Fig.* 7.1 can be used to show the difficulties arising from this approach. People will still wish to free-ride, if they can. So they will attempt to conceal their preferences (in a private good or commercial market situation the act of purchase reveals them). Thus although at Q' the optimal solution to raise marginal taxes of T_1, T_2 and T_3 from each individual respectively (where $T_1 + T_2 + T_3 = P$), and although Q' is the desired goal of all, it is clear that if people believe their share of total taxes will be based on their desire for the good then they will understate that desire to minimise their tax bills and hope, again, to free-ride. This difficulty may be viewed as real but practically unsurmountable unless somehow the good can be privately supplied and the Coase theorem invoked.

Another, and more difficult case, is not only when people have genuinely different marginal valuations of the good, but also when agreement on the optimal quality and the optimal tax is impossible because of this (quite apart from any free-riding propensity or the practical difficulty of determining individual demand curves). This can occur with defence expenditures where pacifists would, under no circumstances, willingly support the military.

It can also occur with less obvious goods. Consider government expenditure on an airport (this is not strictly a public good, but it has some of the characteristics; the provision of travel facilities for other people also results in them being provided for oneself). In *Fig.* 7.2 a two-consumer commodity has a demand for an airport as shown. Individual 2, a salesman, is a frequent traveller. Individual 1, an infrequent traveller but a keen gardener, with a house in the vicinity of the proposed airport, does not value the airport highly at all, given the noise and inconvenience it will cause him compared with the slight benefits which might accrue to him. Moreover, individual 1 has a much higher income than individual 2 and knows that, in reality, his marginal tax rate is related to his income and not to his preferences for public goods of whatever nature. If their marginal tax rates are T_1 and T_2 respectively then, given the two marginal valuation curves, the marginal values of the new airport to individuals 1 and 2 exceeds their marginal costs up to Q_1 and Q_2 units of airport (or flight arrivals or other subdivision).

Unfortunately, an airport is indivisible and both individuals must benefit from and pay for the chosen size of airport. With normal tax

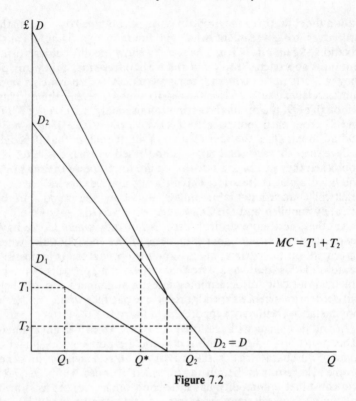

Figure 7.2

structures disagreement is inevitable, irrespective of preference distortion for public relations purposes. Moreover, neither party would be satisfied with the social optimum, Q^*, albeit that is the only output that both individuals could desire and still collectively pay a tax covering the cost of the good. Thus individuals 1 and 2 would desire the public good—airport, national defence, industrial subsidies on whatever—up to the apparently, and probably factually, irreconcilable levels of Q_1 and Q_2. This is a major advantage of private goods and of any attempts to internalise so-called externalities; namely that polarisation of opinions and social disharmonies are minimised and individual diversity is permitted and accommodated.

154

THE ECONOMICS OF BUREAUX

How do civil servants and politicians react when they are given, or they assume, the responsibility for provision of a public good? Here we will examine explicitly the bureaucrat. We will also depart from the strict definition of a 'public good' to examine simply bureaucratic behaviour in the case of a 'publicly provided good'. That is we are interested here in the behaviour of what Mises termed 'bureaucratic management' and in how it differs from 'profit management'. We are concerned with the problem of public goods.

Mises (1966, pp303–11) defined bureaucratic management as 'the method applied in the conduct of administrative affairs, the result of which has no cash value in the market'. Under profit management considerable authority is delegated and so flexibility permitted. The lower levels are expected to know the condition of supply and demand, the particular markets, far better than managers at the top level can possibly know them. Thus there is an integration of knowledge. The top level assigns the general goals while the lower levels attempt to fulfil these goals as profitably as possible. If they succeed they are left alone or rewarded; if they fail they can inform the upper levels of any corrections needed in overall goals, or else they can be replaced. Their income is therefore dependent on success or failure in the market.

Bureaucratic management operates under a totally different method of financing. Expenses are met by the state; thus the responsibility of managers is to see to it that all income received is spent only on those items budgeted for in advance and approved by the sponsor. The discretion of the managers at the various hierarchical levels is not restricted by considerations of profit or loss. They cannot be given the self-understood instruction which need not even be articulated: make profits. If bureaucratic managers were to be given total freedom of action they would do what they wanted, not what their bosses or the people wanted. Mises argues that to 'prevent this outcome . . . it is necessary to give them detailed instructions regulating their conduct of affairs in every respect'. The task of the upper level is supervisory, not in the sense of evaluating profit and loss but in the sense of control. Accurate reporting of control data is at a premium: the goal is total *predictability*.

Predictability as a goal, and the bureaucratic management which aims for it and of itself necessitates it, is neither desirable nor undesirable *per se*. Mises argued that bureaucratic management is indispensable to the conduct ρf affairs which have no cash value on the market. There, profit management is impossible. Entrepreneurship, decision-taking activity to profitably meet the anticipated, but *uncertain*, future demands of consumers, can have no place in an organisation with no cash nexus and a control system which rests on *predictability and certainty*.

Human beings, however, are motivated by self-interest. In a profit-management organisation subject to the take-over threat, this will display itself in entrepreneurial action. As Mises argued, no 'business, whatever its size or specific task, can ever become bureaucratic so long as it is entirely and solely operated on a profit basis'. Should a firm abandon profit-seeking due to an imperfect market in corporate control, however, then bureaucratic management methods will be substituted and entrepreneurship abandoned.

Later writers have developed the analysis still further. For example Niskanen (1971) agrees that there is an important difference between the exchange relation of a public service agency or bureau and that of a market-orientated firm. The bureau offers an all-or-nothing package instead of separate units of services at a price. But Niskanen goes beyond Mises and argues that not only does this preclude entrepreneurial adjustment to the needs of the market, but it also gives it a bargaining power akin to that of a monopoly—profit maximising by discriminating between customers. This results in the bureau producing an output of services larger than a private monopolist would supply. The latter maximises profit, the former maximises total revenue subject to its budget. *Fig.* 7.3 illustrates this argument and shows how the bureau is able to expand output well beyond the competitive ($P=MC$) level.

A competitive industry would produce OD, yielding net consumer benefits of ABC. A bureau, however, because of its all-or-nothing terms of supply and so monopoly bargaining power with politicians (the consumers' elected representatives), can obtain for itself this consumers' surplus. The surplus represents the difference between what consumers (i.e. taxpayers) would be prepared to pay for the good rather than go without the amount bought at the market price. The bureau will, therefore, be able to expand its budget until its output equals OE, twice the optimum, where $CFG = ABC$. This is the 'budget-constrained' case where total revenue or budget ($OBGE$) just covers total costs ($OAFE$). In the 'demand-constrained' case (*Fig.* 7.4)

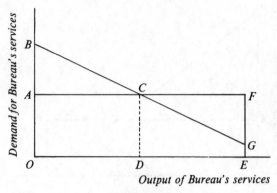

Figure 7.3

bureaux promote their services, shift demand to the right and reduce its elasticity. The bureau will eventually reach a point where the marginal evaluation of its services is zero. In this case the budget (*OBE*) will equal costs (*OAFE*) at output level *E*. Neither situation is optimal, and of the two the less preferred is the demand constrained case. (In *Fig.* 7.4 the ratio of total benefits to total costs for producing the excess output *DE* is *CDE:CDEF*. This is less than the corresponding ratio *CDEG:CDEF* in *Fig.* 7.3.)

Profit managed firms consequently foster entrepreneurship at all levels in the hierarchical firm. The servicing of consumer needs, actual and potential, is a priority and meeting that objective results in entrepreneurial reward. Given the uncertainty involved in the estimation of current and future demand, flexibility is a *sine qua non* at all levels in profit managed organisations. In bureaucratic organisations rigidity of management style is necessary to ensure that consumers do not suffer from opportunism on the part of management below the topmost level. Rigidity of control, however, may not be sufficient to ensure that the incentive for personal gain, which is present in all human beings, does not result in bureaucratic output being expanded beyond the level which the public or consumer would wish. The self-interest which in one case can result in opportunities for creative, consumer-serving, entrepreneurial activity at all levels in a firm can, in the other, result in unwanted levels of 'service' or red tape. In the former, self-interest is channelled into entrepreneurial activity by the casting of a myriad of daily votes by consumers

157

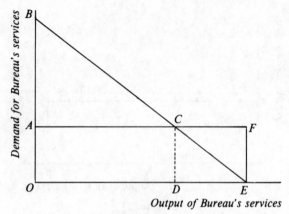

Figure 7.4

through market transactions. In the latter, self-interest is (rightly) curbed on a daily basis by rigid control; but is only curbed (and that inadequately) on an overall scale by infrequent and probably indecisive polling of the electorate.

POLITICS AND VOTING AS MODES OF BUREAUCRATIC CONTROL

Why have we asserted that political control of a bureaucracy is inadequate to achieve maximum consumer welfare? Let us ignore the 'all-or-nothing' nature of public goods and the infrequency of voting as an activity. The answer lies in the motivation of politicians. Just as bureaucrats wish to pursue their own self-interest by expanding their bureaux, the monitor of the bureaucrat, the politician, does so also. He accomplishes this by maximising the votes he can obtain in an election. Unlike the manager, however, who monitors other members of the firm-team and who is in turn controlled by the markets in management personnel and corporate control, this does not result in an outcome catering for the diverse needs of consumers.

This is explained by the *median voter theorem* (Tullock, 1976, pp 14–25). Say there are three voters with different preferences for a given publicly provided good: in ascending order of preference the voters are *A*, *B* and *C*. *B*, the median voter, is the one whose views will be satisfied in a one issue, simple majority voting, political campaign. Should politicians attempt to satisfy A or C respectively, they would not receive the votes of B and C in the former case, nor those of B and A in the latter. This result, of course, means that there is no weight given to the different valuations of A, B and C. All are assumed to have the same strength of feeling about the issue voted on. To the extent that this is so voter disappointment is minimised, but this assumption of homogeneous performance is clearly unrealistic. Thus politicians are not motivated to satisfy the wants of A and C, but rather those of B alone.

In a two party system both parties would compete for the votes of the median voter to achieve election. Thus, for example, parties X and Y would both compete for B's vote, and each would differentiate its appeal to attain A's and C's support respectively) but would do so only trivially (so as not to forfeit B's support).

In a three party system this consensus at the median is less likely. (Tullock, 1976, p23). (This can be illustrated by examining *Figs. 7.5* and *7.6*.) Suppose there are two governmentally provided services, fire and police. Voters such as B may prefer the indicated expenditure on each. Others such as A and C may have different preferences. Assume that voters are distributed evenly over the space. To find how many voters would accept A's, B's and C's preferred policy the total space is divided by inserting the straight line which divides the space into those parts closest to A, B and to C (geometrically the line is midway between A and C and perpendicular to the hypothetical line AC). The median voter theorem suggests the two parties X and Y will cluster together near B in order to split the voters evenly between them. This analysis can be extended to a multi-issue, unevenly distributed voter pattern situation, but the conclusion would remain the same.

In a three party situation the parties, X, Y, and Z need not cluster as indicated in *Fig. 7.6*. If X offers policy X^1 rather than X it will lose votes at the centre of the distribution but, by becoming more 'extreme' will gain votes at the edges. The dashed line shows that in this instance a net gain would be made if Y and Z did not, in turn, alter their policies. Obviously Y and Z will move towards more extreme positions of their own to compensate for this.

Where does this leave the voter? The median voter (or 'average man') is no longer so likely to have his preferences met. Those at the 'extremes' are more or less likely to have their wishes acceded to depending on whether or not their party is in power. Tullock (p24)

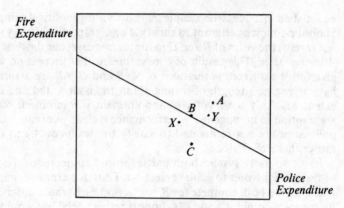

Figure 7.5

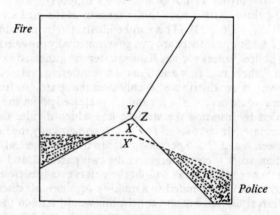

Figure 7.6

alleges that in real life politicians have a more difficult time in assessing how to maximise votes that this theory suggests. Moreover, voter preferences vary in intensity:

> Anyone who has observed real politicians in action can see how they solve the problem. They try to give minority groups with strong preferences in one item (eg agricultural subsidies, trade union protection, industrial subsidies, regional 'aid') favourable treatment in it, and then hope that the group will accept relatively unfavourable treatment in other issues where its feelings are less intense.

Tullock (p24) concludes that this 'analysis of the politician's tactics indicates simply that he is attempting to be re-elected to office, not that he is attempting to maximise the public interest.'

Moreover, Hayek and others have long argued, without the formal analysis of writers such as Tullock, that such an outcome is inevitable. As Hayek (1976, p2) points out 'the public interest . . . cannot consist of the sum of particular satisfactions of the several individuals for the simple reason that neither [the satisfactions] nor all the circumstances determining them can be known to government or anybody else'. Hayek (1976, p7) agrees with Tullock that it is with the interests of particular sectional groups that 'politicians and civil servants are mainly concerned, and that it is through (meeting) them that the former can earn the support of their constituents.' Hayek (p8) neither condemns nor condones this situation but reiterates again that it is inevitable when 'we . . . recall the fundamental facts on which the overall order . . . is based.'

PLANNING: CENTRALISED OR DECENTRALISED?

In brief, since it is individuals not societies which act, it is with individuals, not societies which the study of economics must concern itself. This returns us to the study of catallactics, exchange and competition, and apparently removes us from the *prima facie* rationalism of governmental planning. We have seen that governmental planning is not necessarily planned and benign rationality. Is planning then counterproductive?

Not so argues Hayek. In 1945 (pp519–30) he asked: 'What is the problem we wish to solve when we try to construct a rational economic order?' Given 'all the relevant information', 'a given system of preferences' and 'complete knowledge of available means' the remaining problem is 'purely one of logic'. The answer is implicit in the assumptions. The answer is that the marginal rates of substitution between any two commodities or factors must be the same in all their different issues. But the data from which this calculus starts are never given to a single mind. Thus this cannot be the economic problem since it is insoluble. The knowledge is incomplete, dispersed or contradictory.

The problem is not how to allocate 'given' resources, but rather 'how to secure the best use of resources known to any of the members of society, for ends whose relative importance only these individuals know. It is a problem of the utilisation of knowledge which is not give to anyone in its totality.'

All 'inter-related decisions' about resource allocation, i.e. 'all economic activity', is 'planning'. In any society where planned collaboration occurs, the plans will have to be based on knowledge which initially at least is available to someone other than the planner. In what ways is this knowledge provided to the planner? What is the best way of utilising this knowledge? The former is crucial to an understanding of the economic process. The latter is of importance for economic policy. The answers are linked to the question of '*who* is to do the planning?' This is the area of dispute; not whether planning is to be done or not: but whether centrally (i.e. governmentally), or diffusely. Planning in common terminology usually means central planning, competition simply means decentralised planning. The 'half-way house', 'is the delegation of planning to organised industries' or firms. The more efficient alternative is the one which makes fuller use of existing knowledge, either by putting at the disposal of the central authority all the necessary knowledge currently dispersed; or providing individuals 'such additional knowledge as they need in order to enable them to dovetail their plans with those of others'.

In central planning, Hayek (1945, pp519–30) continues, not only are the 'particular circumstances of time and place' minimised in importance so is 'change'. There are few areas over which central planners and their opponents disagree more strongly than the 'significance and frequency of changes' which will make substantial alterations in production plans necessary. This, of course, makes 'planning' difficult. 'Since economic problems arise always and only in consequence of change.' New plans are not needed so long as things continue as before, or at least as they are expected to. People who minimise the importance of change, are often also those who minimise the extent of the economic problem. Non-Austrian economists have been apt to forget about the constant small changes which make up the economy because of their concentration on aggregates, which, statistically are relatively stable. This stability *cannot* be accounted for by the law of large numbers. The number of elements is not large enough. Rather 'the continuous flow of goods and services is maintained by constant deliberate adjustments, by new dispositions made every day in the light of circumstances not known the day before, by *B* stepping in at once when *A* fails to deliver. Even the large mechanised plant . . .' 'This sort of knowledge . . . cannot be conveyed to any central authority in statistical form.' Statistics of that sort are arrived at by 'abstracting from minor differences', 'by lumping together' items which differ as regards to location, quality, time, place and so on. Decisions based on this knowledge must be left to the 'man on the spot'.

INDIVIDUALISM, COMPETITION AND INFORMATION

If we agree that the economic problem 'is mainly one of rapid adaptation to changes in the particular circumstances of time and place' it follows that decentralisation of decision-making is required. The man on the spot has the intimate knowledge of resources available, changes occurring and of immediate, particular requirements. But his knowledge is limited. Further information must be fed to him so that he can fit his decisions into the whole pattern of changes of the system as a whole. How much knowledge does he need? All has some impact on his situation. But he does not need to know of all events, nor of all their causes or effects, or even why. 'All that is significant to him is *how much more or less* difficult to procure they have become compared with other things with which he is also concerned or how much more or less urgently wanted are the alternative things he produces or uses'.

Now the economic calculus, or the Pure Logic of Choice can be called on, *'at least by analogy'* (emphasis added) to see how this problem is solved by the price system. Even a central planner, with access to the knowledge, would solve the problem by using 'values' or 'rates of equivalence' or MRSs. 'That is, by attaching to each kind of scarce resource a numerical index which cannot be derived from any property possessed by that particular thing, but which reflects, or in which is condensed, its significance in view of the whole means ends structure.'

The price mechanism communicates this information. This function is fulfilled less perfectly the more rigid are prices. 'The most significant fact about this system is the economy of knowledge with which it operates, or how little the individual participants need to know in order to be able to take the right action.' Adjustments made in the light of price changes are probably never 'perfect' in the sense of equilibrium analysis. But the perfect knowledge assumption of that analysis blinds us to the true function of prices, and gives misleading notions of efficiency. The price system is a 'marvel' even if 'normal' rates of return are not always attained, because more of a product is produced, or a raw material used more sparingly as indicated by supply and demand reflected in prices. Man has 'stumbled on' the price system without understanding it. 'Through it not only a division of labour but also a coordinated utilisation of resources based on an equally divided knowledge has become possible.'

Despite the fact that Mises' (1932) view that division of labour depends on the price system was subjected to derision on its original English publication (in 1937), it was soon applauded by Lange and Taylor (in 1938). Hayek (1945, pp519–30) argues that this typifies the apolitical nature of the system. The remaining dissent is restricted primarily to methodological differences. For example, can a Pareto optimum be solved with a massive computer, or with the market? Do consumers by demanding (thus evaluating) consumers' goods *ipso facto* evaluate their factors of production, as Schumpeter (1942, p175) alleged? No, said Hayek. They do not do so literally. Nor do they do so by implication, since 'implication is a logical relationship which can be meaningfully asserted only of propositions simultaneously present to one and the same mind . . . however . . . the values of the factors of production . . . depend . . . also on [their] conditions of supply.' Only if a single mind had all the facts would this implication follow.

But knowledge is dispersed. As Hayek pointed out, if we assume that all the facts are available (for example as to an observing economist with a computer) and so deduce the unique solution assumes away the problem. What 'we must show [is] how a solution is produced by the interactions of people each of whom possesses only partial knowledge.'

An approach such as that of much of mathematical economics with its use of simultaneous equations, 'in effect starts from the assumption that people's *knowledge* corresponds with the objective *facts* of the situation [and] systematically leaves out what is our main task to explain.'

What requires explanation is how the competitive process operates; how and why individuals enter into exchange relationships. But unfortunately the verb 'to compete' and all it implies is meaningless in the mathematical paradigm of perfect competition.

Partly this is because the tautological method which is necessary and appropriate for analysing individual action has been incorrectly extended to the social interaction of many individuals whose decisions influence each other, often sequentially. The conclusions of the economic calculus (the Pure Logic of Choice) are implicit in its assumptions: given-knowledge, available simultaneously to a single mind. The data are not the same for all planning minds in a group. The problem is how the 'data' of these individuals, on which they base their plans, are adjusted to objective external facts, including the actions of others. The calculus can still be used for individuals, but, most importantly changes in the data of different individuals must be included in the process. These changes are brought about by knowledge acquisition. But 'competitive equilibrium' assumes that the data for different individuals are fully adjusted to each other, while the real problem is the process of that adjustment.

Modern competitive equilibrium looks at the effect, not the cause, of the competitive process. Of all the conditions of perfect competition the assumption of complete knowledge of the relevant facts by participants in the market is the most 'critical and obscure' (Hayek, 1976, p95). The assumption cannot be total absolute knowledge and foresight of all facts. This would paralyze all action directed at improvement of our lot. Moreover, nothing is solved by such an assumption. The real problem is how to select and implement the arrangements and institutions necessary to attract the unknown persons who have uniquely useful knowledge to use that knowhow for the relevant task. As Sowell (1980, p3) put it: 'individually we know so pathetically little, and yet socially we use a range and complexity of knowledge that would confound a computer'.

Consider a producer, he is assumed to know the lowest feasible product cost. But it is only through the process of competition that he can gain such knowledge through his success or failure. But perfect competition theory commences with equilibrium and so (Hayek, 1976, p96) 'assumes away the main task which only the process of competition can solve'. Similarly, knowledge of consumer demand cannot be taken as a given, but must be regarded as a problem. Yet, while on the demand side 'such activities as advertising, etc; and the whole organisation of the market serves mainly the need of spreading the information on which the buyer is to act' in perfect competition all such activities implied by the verb 'compete' are excluded. 'Advertising, undercutting, and improving ["differentiating"] the goods or services produced are all excluded by definition.' (Hayek 1976, p96) Most remarkable of all, says Hayek, is the exclusion of individual human actions to gather information. He cites Stigler's *Theory of Price* (1946, p24): 'Economic relationships are never perfectly competitive if they involve any personal relationships between economic units.' This totally conflicts with reality where knowledge is gleaned by experience, and 'competition is in a large measure competition for reputation or goodwill, [this] is one of the most important facts which enables us to solve our daily problems'. In short, competition is here to 'teach us *who* will serve us well' (Hayek, 1976, p97). Lack of supplier similarity does not mean competition is less intense, 'but merely that any degree of competition between them will not produce exactly those results which it would if their services were exactly alike'. To talk of this as a competitive defect can lead to 'absurd conclusions' (p97).

But while the perfect knowledge assumption may appear the most artificial one, it is partly a consequence of another assumption. Namely that of large numbers of firms producing homogeneous commodities, with the same objective facilities for so doing. This gives plausibility to the perfect knowledge assumption. Homogeneity, however, even between distinct markets does not exist. Market boundaries are blurred and even if they were not, plants are located differently. How these differences of supply and demand are reconciled is part of the economic problem, to assume them away provides no answer.

Why then do we not turn to '*compulsory* standardisation'? Hayek (1976, p99) argues this on individualistic grounds: 'this is something very different from the demands of those who believe that the variety of people's tastes should be disregarded and the constant experimentation with improvements should be suppressed in order to obtain the advantages of perfect competition.' The yardstick ought to be 'the situation as it would exist if competition were prevented from operating' (p100). For example, the different things would not be produced by those who know best how to do so, and so at least cost, and all the things that consumers want would also fail to be produced. There would be little relationship between price and lowest cost. Moreover, the solution is always 'a voyage of exploration into the unknown', as attempts are made 'to discover new ways of doing things better' (p101). As long as the economic problem exists, viz 'unforeseen changes which require adaptation' this will be so.

This all epitomises non-Austrian theory's neglect of the time element:

> If we think of it, as we ought to, as a succession of events, it becomes even more obvious that in real life there will at any moment be as a rule only one producer who can manufacture a given article at the lowest cost and who may in fact sell below the cost of his next successful competitor, but who, while still trying to extend his market, will often be overtaken by somebody else, who in turn will be prevented from capturing the whole market by yet another, and so on. Such a market would clearly never be in a state of perfect competition, yet competition in it might not only be as intense as possible but would also be the essential factor in bringing about the fact that the article in question is supplied at any moment to the consumer as cheaply as this can be done by any known method. (Hayek, 1976, p102).

If we compare this sort of 'imperfect' market with a 'perfect' market such as grain we can see the distinction between the underlying, objective facts of a situation, which cannot be altered by a firm's activities, (or a consumer's), and the competitive activities themselves, by which men adapt to the situation. In the latter there is 'little need or scope' for competitive activity, because the situation which such activity might bring about already exists. Knowledge of any change diffuses so rapidly, and is adapted to so quickly, that what happens during the transition is usually disregarded and study confined to comparison of equilibria. But it is this neglected interval, and the forces operating in it which must be studied 'if we are to "explain" the equilibrium which follows it'. Where adaptation is slow the process of competition is continuous. This process (with free entry) may secure no more than a temporary supply of goods and services for which there is an effective demand at the least current expenditure of resources in the given historical situation. And even though the price is considerably higher and only just below the cost of the next best way of satisfying a consumer's need, this 'is more than we can expect from any other known system' (p105). 'The decisive point is still the elementary one that it is most unlikely that, without [entry barriers], any commodity or service will for any length of time be available only at a price at which outsiders could expect a more than normal profit if they entered the field.' (Hayek, 1976, p.105). So 'we should worry much less about whether competition in a given case is perfect and worry much more about whether there is competition at all'. More will be learnt about competition's significance by studying the effects of its deliberate suppression than by concentrating on the shortcomings of the actual situation compared with an unattainable 'ideal'. Suppression is also more critical than absence, since total absence is unlikely in natural conditions, without the tolerance or assistance of government.

Thus Hayek endorses again the notion that competition can solve the economic problem of the division of knowledge. The fact that humans are individuals with unique knowledge stocks results in the economic problem. Competition can solve the problem. *Centralised* control can suppress but not solve it. For Austrians this effectively restricts the argument to the undesirability of *government* as opposed to general central planning (since a *private* centralised monopoly based on superior efficiency in meeting consumer needs does little harm provided its disappearance is assured by the threat of rivalrous entry). Only government can erect entry barriers which (by law or force) cannot be circumvented by clever entrepreneurs.

Thus we have seen reiterated again an emphasis on individualism in Austrian economics. Does this mean Austrianism has an underlying set of moral values, or can it be regarded, as some economists claim of the neo-classical approach, to be value free? It is to this question we now turn.

✦

REFERENCES

R H Coase, 'The Problem of Social Cost', *Journal of Law and Economics*, Vol. 4, (1961) pp1–49.

S Cheung, *The Myth of Social Cost*, Hobart Paper No 82, Institute of Economic Affairs, (1978).

F A Hayek, 'The Use of Knowledge in Society', *American Economic Review*, (1945).

F A Hayek, *The Constitution of Liberty*, Routledge, Kegan Paul, (1976).

D Hume *A Treatise on Human Nature*, Clarendon Press, (1960).

O Lange and F M Taylor, 'On the Economic Theory of Socialism' in *On the Economic Theory of Socialism*, D E Lippincott (ed), University of Minnesota Press, (1938).

L von Mises, *Human Action*, Henry Regnery, (1966).

L Mises, *Die Gemeinwirtschaft,* (1932). (Published as *Socialism* in 1937).

W R Niskanen, *Bureaucracy and Representative Government*, Aldine-Atherton (1971).

Politics, Bureaucracy and Commercialism

P A Samuelson, *Economics* McGraw-Hill (1976 edn).
J Schumpeter, *Capitalism, Socialism and Democracy*, Harper and Row, (1942).
G J Stigler, *The Theory of Price*, Macmillan, (1946).
T A Sowell, *Knowledge and Decisions*, Basic Books, (1980).
G Tullock, *The Vote Motive*, Hobart Paper No 9, Institute of Economic Affairs, (1976).

8 The Morals and Ethics of Austrianism

In previous chapters we have seen that individualism is highly regarded by Austrians as a means of solving the problems of economic calculation. Central governmental planning is perceived as being unable in practice to do so. Only the price system, set in motion by entrepreneurial activity can achieve our goals. Moreover it does so, so claim Austrians, more effectively, even in the presence of mistakes or errors, than the centrally planned alternative. In addition, these views are consistent with the Austrian methodology of praxeology, that man purposefully acts in order to achieve his goals. It is not surprising, therefore, to find that Austrian economists generally are not collectivists in their political and moral views. Some, such as Rothbard (1978) are anarchists in that they see little or no role for the state. Others, like Hayek (1976) see a limited role for centralised authority, while Kirzner (1975) discusses morality and justice in general without revealing his stance. All, however, would align themselves with Mises (1981, pp1–12) where he argued that the great 'problem is whether or not socialism should supplant the market economy'. They would agree with his ultimate conclusion that it should not. They would also sympathise with Hayek, who in the foreword to the Mises' book (1981, p xix) related how he first read it shortly after World War I, in the 1920s when '[s]ocialism promised to fulfil all our hopes for a more rational, more just world. And then came this book. Our hopes were dashed.'

Readers of the past few chapters will not be surprised by any of the above. They may, however, remain unaware of how Mises (1981, pp1–12) defined socialism. He includes communists, Christian socialists, social democrats, democratic socialists, Nazis, Fascists, 'New Dealers', welfare statists and so on. Socialism thus embraces a large number of moral codes, antipathetic to Austrian economics. Austrians, conversely can be labelled as (in Europe) liberals or Whigs, (in America) as libertarians, as anarchists or, to use Mises' less emotive phraseology, as market economists. The next few pages attempt to briefly justify and explain this Austrian stance.

THE IMPOSSIBILITY OF SOCIALIST CALCULATION.

It is many years since Mises' *Socialism* first argued against the possibility of central economic planning. The previous chapters have summarised some of the ensuing literature from the pen of Mises himself, and later from Hayek and Kirzner. In this section we examine the sole 'refutation' of Mises' claim (by Lange and Taylor (1938)) and find it wanting.

Lange and Taylor's 'refutation' occupies only two pages of their essay (pp59–61) and commences by arguing that Mises' argument that socialist calculation cannot solve the allocation problem of economics 'is based on [his] confusion concerning the nature of prices'. What was this alleged confusion? Lange and Taylor (citing Wicksteed) say correctly that price has two meanings: a narrow and a general. The narrow is 'the exchange ratio of two commodities on a market', this is the money price. But this is only a special case of the 'generalised meaning of "terms on which alternatives are offered".' Lange and Taylor continue: '[it] is only prices in the generalised sense which are indispensable to solving the problem of the allocation of resources.'

This is true and Wicksteed was correct. But Lange and Taylor are not correct to impugn to Mises the belief that individuals do not balance alternatives within their range of knowledge. Rather, as Hayek (1982, p135) points out, the fact that the terms on which alternatives are offered 'become known to us in most instances only as *money* prices is Mises' chief argument' (emphasis in original).

Lange and Taylor go on:

The economic problem is a problem of choice between alternatives. To solve the problem three data are needed: (a) a preference scale which guides the acts of choice; (b) knowledge of the terms on which alternatives are offered; (c) knowledge of the amount of resources available. Those three data being given, the problem of choice is soluble.

Lange and Taylor then assert (with no intervening text) that 'it is *obvious* [emphasis added] that a Socialist economy may regard the

171

data under (a) and (c) as given, at least in as great a degree as they are given in a Capitalist economy'. How the millions of pieces of dispersed information relating to preferences and resources in an economy at any point in time can ever be given is not explained. One statement, and that a *non-sequitur* relates to point (a), and none at all to point (c). 'The data under (a) may be either given by the demand schedules of the individuals *or be established by the judgement* of the authorities administering the . . . system' (emphasis added). How the latter mode can be regarded as providing given data defies the bounds of logic, and how the former mode does so requires an understanding of how demands are revealed by acting consumers and producers in the market place.

Lange and Taylor continue:

the question remains whether the data under (b) are accessible to the administrators of a Socialist economy. Professor von Mises denies this. However, a careful study of price theory and of the theory of production convinces us that, the data under (a) and under (c) being given, the terms on which alternatives are offered can be determined.

This, of course is true. The theoretician with knowledge of (a) and (c) *can* determine the point where the marginal rates of substitution of any two commodities or factors will be the same in all their different uses. But that is not the issue. The issue is that neither the administrators in a Socialist economy nor the entrepreneurs in a capitalist one have knowledge of the data under (a) and (c) (which a price theorist, if available, could then apply to obtain (b)). What capitalist entrepreneurs do have is *market prices as surrogates* for (b), on which they can then act to satisfy perceived demands from perceived resources. And this they do for the millions of different demands more promptly and more accurately than the Socialist alternative (even if its existence was possible) since the plethora of information does not need to be gathered together and processed in one central place but needs only to be collated and acted upon by entrepreneurs close (whether in spatial or other terms) to the specific demands and idiosyncratic sources in question. The argument is stronger still when changing preferences and resources are introduced.

Specificity, idiosyncracy and time render Lange and Taylor's given knowledge of (a) and (c) a meaningless abstraction in reality. Mises' use of market prices as a surrogate for (b) is the only workable alternative for directing resources (c) to their most highly valued uses (a). It is not a 'theoretically perfect' alternative, it is open to errors and mistakes which a theoretical model is not. But, to Austrians it is closer to perfection than the only practical alternative: dictatorially determined resource direction and consumption patterns.

Yet Lange and Taylor do not distinguish between theoretical ideals and practical possibilities. As a consequence they miss the main thrust of the argument that market prices (b) reveal information about unknown and unknowable demands (a) and unknown and unknowable supplies (c). Rather they confuse cause and effect by claiming that since (a) and (c) are known (b) can be calculated. Thus they say, again without substantiation of their own, that the 'administrators of the socialist economy will have exactly the same knowledge . . . as the [capitalists] have'. But since entrepreneurs are, in fact informed solely by market prices the planners, in the absence of market prices and with no 'given data', would be in total ignorance.

THE MORAL JUSTIFICATION OF THE MARKET ECONOMY

Free and voluntary trade and exchange results in net benefits to both parties to the trade. Trade is initiated by entrepreneurship stimulated by perceived price differentials. If the entrepreneur errs in a trading transaction only he loses, a possibility he willingly accepted. His incentive not to err is the spur of profit and loss. Thus in a market economy the information that two parties wish to trade is conveyed by price differentials, the motivation which encourages the entrepreneur to facilitate the trade is the presence of profit.

In a non-market, or socialist economy, the information is no longer conveyed by market prices (since they do not exist to the extent that the socialist administrators have compromised their principles and either use prices from markets in foreign countries as a proxy, or permit decentralised markets to operate and generate price information in defiance of socialist dogma). Decisions are taken, therefore, based on facts or opinions which do not and cannot reflect the individual wishes of society members. The motivation to take allocation decisions is not profit but bureaucratic and/or political power. Thus, depending on the constraints placed on the decision-takers by the nature of the socialist system under study, the decisions will favour to a greater or lesser degree, those segments of society which are perceived to be best placed to bolster and preserve the power and authority of the relevant bureaucrats and politicians.

This neither will be nor can be in the interests of the individual members of society as they would reveal those interests to be in their preference schedules or demand curves whilst acting and choosing freely. The decision-takers do not have the required information and their incentive system is not compatible with that information should they have it.

These arguments are not arguments against the use of 'economic planning'. The issue is rather who are the decision-makers who are to do the planning? When politicians refer to economic planning they mean as Sowell (1980, p214) points out, the *'forcible superseding of other people's plans* by government officials' (emphasis is original). By so doing, government planning dispenses with the price system as a device for economising on a scarce and diffuse resource, knowledge, and so ignores or tramples over individual rights.

There are two issues here: one is minor, the other (from a moral stance) is fundamental. The minor issue is whether or not individual planning (at personal, household or firm level) is liable to error, either more or less, than forcible planning. The major issue is whether forcible planning is compatible with individual liberty. We will now examine these issues in turn.

ERROR IN ECONOMICS

One simplistic and common-sense view of economic error is that centralised planning is either 'all right' or 'all wrong' while decentralised planning will result in an outcome which is never 'all wrong'. For this reason decentralisation is to be preferred.

However, as we have observed over the last few chapters neither orthodox neo-classical economists nor socialist economists would accept this common-sense approach. Both would argue that perfect knowledge is present or accessible to the relevant decision makers. Austrians reject the perfect knowledge assumption (although not the rationality postulate which normally goes with it). Mises (1957, p268) argues that to 'make mistakes in pursuing one's ends is a widespread human weakness . . . Error, inefficiency and failure must not be confused with irrationality.' Such failure may simply be the result of greater or lesser degree of competence.

Does this return Austrians to the 'all-or-nothing' common sense view of centralised versus decentralised planning? A negative answer must also be given to this question. Kirzner (1979, pp131-6) points out that economics not only permits error, but it *depends* on error. He cites Jevons' Law of Indifference that 'in the same open market, at any one moment, there cannot be two prices for the same kind of article.' Jevons' Law underlies the whole competitive process of the tendency for divergent prices to converge. There is a 'tendency for imperfect knowledge to be replaced by more perfect knowledge'. This spontaneous tendency exists because 'the lure of available pure profits can be counted upon to alert at least some market participants' or entrepreneurs into action. This analysis enables Kirzner to align Austrian thought with aspects of Liebenstein's notion of X-inefficiency. X-inefficiency exists if the producer is inside the 'outer-bound production possibility surface consistent with [his] resources' (Liebenstein, 1966, p413). Such a situation reflects error and as yet uncovered entrepreneurial opportunities.

Ten years later Stigler (1976) criticised Liebenstein's concept of X-inefficiency as being simply a description of inadequacy of motivation and effort by members of firms which can be embraced in the neoclassical framework. Kirzner (1979, p127) agrees with this Stiglerian view but does not accept that Liebenstein's concept is limited in this way only to motivational deficiency. If individuals prefer leisure to working harder, or if they prefer expending less effort rather than more on searching for information as to how to reach their production possibility frontier then deliberate and 'correct' error-free Stiglerian choices have been made. Errors have not occurred. Errors *have* occurred, however, if the individuals concerned would have reproached themselves *at the time* for taking the course of action they did in the light of the knowledge available to (but not perceived by) them at the time. This type of error is due to absence of entrepreneurial alertness and a by-passing of extant, available opportunities. (It is *not* the by-passing of opportunities whose existence can only become known with the passage of time.)

As Kirzner indicates, however, Stigler's critique is only valid in an equilibrium framework. If firms do have different costs in equilibrium then this can be attributed to differing input qualities (for example personnel with a lower motivation). These cost differences are not attributable to error. But if one moves from equilibrium to Jevons' Law of Indifference which suggests rather a tendency to converge towards equilibrium then 'scope exists for entrepreneurial activity' (p134) and cost differences can be attributed either to qualitative input variations or to lack of alertness and so error.

As soon as genuine error is allowed into the analysis then no simplistic judgement can be made that decentralised planning is better or worse than 'all-or-nothing' central planning. (Over time even central planning decisions need not be 'all- or- nothing'; they can be revised.) Rather the analysis must proceed by way of questioning which form of economic planning is more likely to prompt error eliminating entrepreneurship: a profit-motivated society or an economy where political gain is a prime driving force? Neither 'common-sense' nor 'equilibrium-oriented, error-free' economics can answer this question.

JUSTICE, RIGHTS AND ENTITLEMENTS.

There is little doubt as to how Austrian economists would answer the preceding question. They would appeal to either *a priori* reasoning or to the verdict of history. Nevertheless in the final analysis Austrian economists would justify their moral and ethical stance not on maximising material well-being by choosing the system which best facilitates market adjustments but on theories on natural human rights.

The writers on whom Austrians drew for their inspiration on property, human rights and freedom range from Locke in the seventeenth century (Locke, 1967) to Mill in the nineteenth (Mill, 1947) and most recently Nozick (1974). If Jevons' Law of Indifference is to hold, if prices do indeed have a tendency to converge as entrepreneurial alertness facilitates trade and exchange the basic moral question is raised: 'how does one obtain an entitlement to that which is traded'? Such an entitlement is a prerequisite for voluntary, non-coerced exchange.

Nozick (1974, p ix) states that '[i]ndividuals have rights, and there are things no person or group may do to them [without violating their rights]'. Nozick draws heavily on Locke's 'state of nature' where, citing Locke, Nozick (1974, p10) argues individuals are in 'a state of perfect freedom to order their actions and dispose of their possessions and persons as they think fit, within the bounds of the law of nature' which requires that 'no one ought to harm another in his life, health, liberty or possessions'.

It is axiomatic in the Lockean theory of property that human beings are self-owners. From this Nozick develops his entitlement theory (1974 p151):

'If the world were wholly just, the following inductive definition would exhaustively cover the subject of justice in holdings.
1. A person who acquires a holding in accordance with the principle of justice in acquisition is entitled to that holding.
2. A person who acquires a holding in accordance with the principle of justice in transfer, from someone else entitled to the holding, is entitled to the holding.
3. No one is entitled to a holding except by (repeated) application of 1 and 2'.

As a self-owner, each individual has a right or entitlement to the labour services he performs using his human capital. All other rights are the consequences or corollaries of this one. It is misleading to call this self-ownership or labour services right the 'right to life' (Rand, 1967, p322). The right to life as Nozick pointed out (1974, p179) could imply the right to certain physical things necessary to sustain life, but if other people have rights over these physical things then their rights are violated. To be fair to Rand she does not define the right to life in this way, although the phrase would seem to imply it. Rather she is consistent with Locke claiming (p322) that it is:

. . . the right to engage in self-sustaining and self-generated action . . . for the furtherance, the fulfilment and the enjoyment of [one's] own life . . . a right is the moral sanction of a positive—of . . . freedom to act on [one's] own judgment, for [one's] own goals, by [one's] own *voluntary, uncoerced* choice. As to [one's] neighbours, [one's] rights impose no obligations on them except of a negative kind: to abstain from violating [one's] rights. (Emphasis in original).

This notion of self-ownership is completely consistent with Böhm-Bawerk's view (p63 above) that the worker is entitled to a wage equivalent to the full value of what he produces. But so far we have only examined labour as a factor of production. How can we now introduce land and capital into the Lockean theory of rights and into Nozick's entitlement theory?

According to Locke an individual gets an entitlement to a previously unowned gift of nature by being the first person to mix his labour with that piece of land. The right to (unowned) land arises by mixing it with what is owned (labour), thereby removing the gift of nature from its original state and putting into a state more serviceable to human wants (i.e. into capital or even into a first order good).

For most cases this is a sufficient theory of property and property rights. But what of extremes? Or, to put it another way, do property rights also imply duties or obligations? Nozick (p175–82) cites several such: a castaway arriving at a desert island which someone had already appropriated would apparently have no right to land; an owner of the only water hole in a desert can apparently charge what he will to thirsty travellers; a man who mixes a glass of tomato juice with the ocean becomes the apparent owner of the ocean, or has the action simply resulted in the waste of a glass of juice? The Lockean proviso that there be 'enough and as good left in common for others' is meant, according to Nozick (p175), to satisfy the '*crucial point* [as to] whether appropriation of an unowned object worsens the situation of others' (emphasis added).

Thus Nozick (pp175–82) would argue that the tomato juice is wasted, the waterhole owner cannot charge what he likes and the castaway cannot be turned away from the island. This he justifies on the grounds of Locke's 'proviso' although he admits (p180) this makes it 'difficult any longer unreservedly to call' something a person's property. Thus duties and obligations do indeed appear to arise from property rights, but in so doing dilute the concept of rights themselves.

This is somewhat unsatisfactory and leaves the discussion indeterminate. People are self-owners. They add to that property by mixing their labour with unowned land to create their own first or higher order goods. Consequently, if they engage in voluntary and uncoerced trade and exchange (see Nozick's point 2, p177) the property rights are transferred. But the property rights are only valid if they do not run afoul of the Lockean proviso. For the vast majority of cases they will not but for a few extremes and situations where a duty exists towards someone other than oneself they will.

Nozick's examination of the principles of transfer and their justice is limited to emphasising the voluntariness of exchange and total lack of compulsion and fraud in the execution of the trade. Kirzner (1979, pp200–24) argues that this results in his ignoring the fact that trade occurs because an entrepreneur has discovered that differing valuations exist between a willing buyer and a willing seller. Moreover such differing valuations exist if any and all trades are to take place and not merely a few exceptional ones such as the sale of a glass of water to a thirsty desert traveller.

In short, different valuations by traders imply (excluding fraud and compulsion) a universal presence in all trading of a certain degree of error. 'Those who paid the higher prices were clearly unaware of the sellers who were prepared to accept, and in fact did accept, lower prices', and *vice versa* (Kirzner, 1979, p204). If most market transactions depend on this type of valuation 'error' how can their 'voluntariness' and hence the 'justice' of the outcome be defended? (The glass of water in the desert is simply an extreme case of such error in that the prudent traveller no doubt first ascertained that the desert had ample oases when he first set out on his journey: he simply had no inkling, that, for whatever reason, his projections were wrong. Similarly the value the castaway placed on being allowed to set foot on the desert island when he commenced his original and apparently secure sea-journey would be very low. He might even have had no idea the island was there and so placed no value on it at all.)

Kirzner argues that it is possible to disentangle the validity of rights (and so their independence from obligations) from this apparent impasse. The dilemma is that all transactions, not just a few extreme exceptions are dependent on mistakes made by the traders but uncovered by the entrepreneur. All trades thus appear to contradict both the Lockean proviso of not making others worse off and paradoxically, the condition of voluntariness: since the trades would not have been made had both parties been fully informed. To do so Kirzner (1979, p218) points out that Nozick's entitlement theory (1974, p151) is not 'exhaustive' as claimed. It is based on acquisition from nature and acquisition by transfer. An intermediate category of 'finders-creators *ex nihilo*-keepers' is required (Kirzner, p218).

But to:

introduce plausibility into the notion of finders-keepers, [one must] adopt the view that, until a resource has been discovered, *it has not*, in the sense relevant to the rights of access and common use, *existed at all* . . . the discoverer . . . in the relevant sense [is] the creator of what he [has] found (p212) (emphasis in the original).

From this one can deduce that entrepreneurial alertness of a profit opportunity or price differential 'constitutes the discovery of hitherto unknown and non-existent value' (p214). The alertness by an entrepreneur to price differences can range from different prices for the same good in two different places, or at two different times in the same place, or more completely to perceiving that a mixture of resources, if brought together can result in a final product with a much higher duly time discounted, money price than the original resource bundle. The two latter are 'constructing the future' and approaching the 'heroic' entrepreneur of Schumpeterian literature. All are creating value where none existed before (if they have guessed correctly) and profit thereby, but if they fail to create this value (by guessing incorrectly) only they, the entrepreneurs lose. The Lockean proviso is not violated if the finders-keepers ethic of acquisition is introduced into Nozick's entitlement theory.

This enables one to tackle Nozick's problematic exceptions. The owner of the water hole in the desert and of the castaway's island have undoubted property rights over them. Whatever the source of the alertness which resulted in their acquiring these resources the point is that no other desert travellers nor sea-voyagers displayed similar alertness, albeit some, at some time, must have had the same opportunities. These latter are no worse off as a result of the mistaken decisions they took at the same time as the current oasis and island owners. In fact, they may even become better off, *in the event*, since the sources of the means of saving their lives may now have to attract their attention. The desert travellers (whose alertness was less than the entrepreneurs at the start of the journey) may be even less entrepreneurially alert when suffering from thirst. They may have to receive messages from the water hole owner, acting as an entrepreneur by proxy on their behalf, to let them know water is available a short distance away. Hence advertising its justification. And by carrying out one's duty to oneself by negotiating a voluntary exchange with another, one's 'duties' to them (as some would term them) are fulfilled. The thirst of the traveller is quenched.

What of the waterhole owner who refuses to part with water except at a price ruinous for the drinker? This writer and his readers might well have serious moral reservations about such behaviour. Nevertheless, the owner has still not violated the Lockean proviso to Nozick's entitlement theory when the finders-creators-keepers means of just acquisition is included. He is still the just owner of the water hole. To be intellectually consistent one must concede his absolute right to the oasis. Nonetheless, in practice, many individuals receive personal satisfaction from charitable actions. Furthermore, those who would not act 'morally' in such a situation would soon be relieved of their monopoly by new entrepreneurial market entrants.

Even with such moral reservations for extreme cases the Austrian economist still prefers diffusion of decision-making to centralisation. A centrally taken decision (backed by the power of government: the only legal monopolist of force) cannot be changed except by force or a change in governmental values. Thus if it is decided that all desert travellers be banned from the waterhole, or Jews from food and jobs as by Hitler, or Kulaks from land as by Stalin, little can be done about it. Entry by other entrepreneurs to the relevant market is (legally) impossible. But as Kirzner (1973, p99) points out, '*with respect to purely entrepreneurial activity no possible obstacles to freedom of entry can exist*' (emphasis in original). Thus while a private monopolist could ban travellers from his waterhole, he could not, however, ban other entrepreneurs flying in water, laying a pipeline, or devising a swifter means of travel across the desert. Since entrepreneurship does not require access to any particular *specific resource*, entry and monopoly removal cannot be impeded. But if *resources in general* are not privately owned, but rather are controlled by the state, then entrepreneurial entry into the market for quenching or preventing the thirst of desert travellers is impossible. The issue is therefore not principally one of property rights. But rather a question of which political climate will encourage mutually beneficial entrepreneurial exchange. To Austrians Mises' anti-socialist analyses provide the answer.

WEALTH AND REDISTRIBUTION

To the extent that the current distribution of income and wealth is justified by Lockean theory can a case be made for redistribution of that income and wealth? The answer given by almost all economists is an unqualified 'yes'. Only Mises (1966, p807) has come out strongly against this position:

Taxes are necessary. But the system of discriminatory taxation universally accepted under the misleading name of progressive taxation of income and inheritance is not a mode of taxation. It is rather a mode of disguised expropriation of the successful capitalists and entrepreneurs.

There are two reasons why Mises stands in virtual isolation over this issue. The first is due to the near universal abandonment of their own discipline by all economists on this issue in favour of apparent 'common-sense'. The second is due to a confusion of income and wealth.

The first is a consequence of a misuse of the marginal utility doctrine. Believers in a progressive income tax originally argued that since each additional unit of money income is worth less to the recipient then the preceding one then a progressive tax makes sense. This is because the goods bought by the nth income unit of a low earner are valued more highly than the goods bought by the $100n^{th}$ income unit of a higher earner. The high earner will have purchased all those goods and services high on his value scale long before he receives his $100n^{th}$ income unit. Thus total social utility can be improved by transferring through taxation some of his income and giving it to the lower earner. It was not until Robbins (1935, Chapter 6) argued that while it was valid for an individual to rank the values of each income unit he received, it was not legitimate to make interpersonal comparisons. The high income earner may well value his last unit of income very highly indeed while the low earner may not (for example, one may be a glutton, the other an ascetic). Subjective utilities cannot be compared. This view is now comprehensively accepted by economists in theory but rejected by them in favour of 'common-sense' in practice. As Hayek (1976, p517, n10) pointed out, this is because:

individually most of us have definite views about whether a given need of one person is greater or smaller than that of another. [But] the fact that we have an opinion . . . in no way implies that there is an objective basis for deciding who is right . . . nor . . . [are we] likely to agree.

Hayek (1976, pp318–9) also highlights the second reason a progressive income tax is universally favoured. It is due to the failure to distinguish between income and wealth. Most people are what he calls 'salaried men' rather than entrepreneurial capitalists. To the former:

current net receipts are normally intended for current consumption . . . [which is a notion] alien to the thinking of those whose aim is to build up a business . . . [rather for them] profits and losses are mainly a mechanism for redistributing capital . . . [from the less successful to the successful not] a means of providing their current sustenance.

And, of course, since government policy aims to satisfy most of us (salaried men) in the short electoral run, rather than training us about the role of the entrepreneur in ever better satisfying our wants over a persistent period of time, progressive income tax is apparently logical and common-sensical, however much it contradicts Locke's and Nozick's property rights theories. Moreover, there is no pay-off to government in the latter course of action so its legislative behaviour in this matter is perfectly rational.

James Meade (1948, p40) in a book otherwise containing a defence of progressive taxation highlights some absurdities which it can give rise to and their impact upon society's wealth enhancing division of labour:

Thus a skilled author who is taxed (at 97.5%) in the £ must earn £200 . . . to have . . . £5 to get some housework done. He may well decide to do the housework himself instead of writing. Only if he is forty times more productive in writing than in housework will it be profitable for him to (do otherwise).

AUSTRIANISM IN A NUTSHELL

Nozick (1974, p160) unwittingly summarises the morals and ethics of Austrian economics in a clumsy sentence as follows:

From each according to what he chooses to do, to each according to what he makes for himself (perhaps with the contracted aid of others) and what others choose to do for him and choose to give him of what they've been given previously (under this maxim) and haven't yet expended or transferred.

He condenses this into the aphorism: (emphasis in original).

'*From each as they choose, to each as they are chosen*' (emphasis in original).

FINAL THOUGHTS

In many economic treatises the concluding section is headed 'Policy Conclusions'. Clearly such a sub-title would be inappropriate here. As we have seen Austrians argue for minimal government and so minimal policy intervention. The unanswered question from the above pages, however, is just how minimalist should government be? Some Austrians (for example Rothbard) are total anarchists. Others, such as Hayek, would argue for a specified role, as for example where public goods and externalities exist (Hayek has thus come out in favour of governmental support for agricultural research).

Others might argue that government is merely required to 'hold the ring' while property rights become defined. (As was the case with the Homestead Act of the mid-nineteenth century in the American West). Once these are defined the Coase Theorem suggests the role of government then ceases. But the implications of transaction cost theory could suggest the reverse.

Literature on the economics of politics and bureaus, however, hints that even with transaction costs as a *raison d'être*, the government will tend to be relatively less efficient (in meeting consumer wants) than the unfettered market and furthermore its consumption of resources will tend to grow in ratchet like fashion.

At the end of the day the reader must make a value judgement and select one of the following premises:

(a) government is redundant and the market can provide goods and services in even 'traditional' areas of law and order;
(b) there is a limited role for government which must be strictly controlled by some political or constitutional means;
(c) Austrian economics has developed well beyond its early beginnings but is still an uncompleted research programme which is still unable to aid us in choosing between (a) or (b);
(d) (and much less ambitiously), Austrian economics should be regarded as an interesting part of intellectual history which has refocussed our attention on the dynamic uncertainty of the economic process in which prices and profits play a vitally important role, but as a research programme its job is complete and the task is now simply to integrate it back into the mainstream.

Whatever the answer, there is no question that after the Austrian resurgence of the last decade, we can return to the condition we were in before Lachmann and others commenced their 'salvage of ideas'.

REFERENCES

F Hayek, *The Constitution of Liberty*, Routledge & Kegan Paul, (1976).

F Hayek, 'Two Pages of Fiction', *Journal of Economic Affairs*, (1982).

I. Kirzner, *Perception, Opportunity and Profit*, University of Chicago Press, (1979).

O Lange, and F M Taylor, 'On the Economic Theory of Socialism' in *On the Economic Theory of Socialism*, D E Lippincott (ed.), University of Minnesota Press, (1938).

H. Liebenstein, Allocative Efficiency vs. X-Efficiency, *American Economic Review*, (1966).

J Locke, *Second Treatise on Government*, P. Laslett (ed), Cambridge University Press, (1967).

J S Mill, *On Liberty* A Castell (ed), Crofts Classics, (1947).

L ·on Mises, *Theory and History*, Yale University Press, (1957).

L von Mises, *Socialism*, Liberty Press, (1981).

R Nozick, *Anarchy, State and Utopia*, Basic Books, (1974).

M Rothbard, *For a New Liberty*, Collier Macmillan, (1978).

A Rand, *Capitalism: The Unknown Ideal*, Signet, (1967).

T A Sowell, *Knowledge and Decisions*, Basic Books, (1980).

G J Stigler, 'The Xistence of X-efficiency', *American Economic Review*, (1976).

Appendix

WHO WERE (OR ARE) THE AUSTRIANS?

The reader may well be forgiven if he is confused by the plethora of names cited above. Who were (or are) these individuals and what positions did they hold?

Carl Menger was Professor of Political Economy at the University of Vienna from 1873 to 1903. Prior to that he had served for a short while in the Austrian civil service.

Böhm-Bawerk, one of Menger's main disciples, died in 1914. He studied law at Vienna University and became a member of the Austrian Government, holding the position of Minister of Finance, three times in a fifteen year period. Born in 1851, Böhm-Bawerk did not become a senior academic until after Menger's death when, in 1904, he was appointed Professor of Economics at Vienna. By that time he had already written his principal works.

Friedrick von Wieser was the other major disciple of Menger. Born in the same year as Böhm-Bawerk he died in 1926. Like Böhm-Bawerk he studied at the University of Vienna and took up a non-prominent government post thereafter. Unlike his colleague he returned to academic life in, respectively, Heidelberg, Leipzig and (as Professor) Prague. In 1903 he succeeded to Menger's chair in Vienna. His main contribution resulted in him being remembered as the first economist to formulate clearly the doctrine of opportunity cost.

The Austria of the 1920s must have crackled intellectually. There *Fritz Machlup* (later Professor in New York University, died 1983), *Friedrich Hayek, Gottfried Haberler, Oscar Morgenstein*, and *Ludwig von Mises* (died 1973) held their famous seminars, inspired first by Wieser and later by Mises.

Ludwig von Mises became Professor of Economics at Vienna from 1931–38 having first worked as economist for the Austrian Chamber of Commerce. By way of Geneva he went to the USA where he took out American citizenship in 1946. His uncompromising intellectual beliefs and antipathy towards socialism of any kind earned him devoted friendships and bitter enmities. He held his now famous weekly seminars at New York University Graduate School of Business. But Mises was ignored by his peers and never, in his quarter of a century at the institution, was he awarded a chair at New York. Indeed his salary was, at least partly, paid by a private foundation. Shunned by his brother economists he was finally awarded a Distinguished Fellowship of the American Economic Association in 1969 at the age of 88. But the testimonial was grudging as was pointed out in his obituary in the 1974 *American Economic Review* (p518).

Of his 16 books, three are milestones. *The Theory of Money and Credit*, 1912, has already been alluded to. *Socialism* appeared ten years later in 1922. There Mises revealed the intellectual poverty of socialist doctrine. To that point no socialist writer, from Marx to the Webbs, had paid any attention to the problem of resource allocation without a price system which would still ensure the outcome desired by the socialist planners (to say nothing of consumer wishes). Finally, his *Human Action*, 1949, provided the capstone to his career. This massive work, subtitled *A Treatise on Economics*, differed in organisation, philosophy, methodology and ideology from any equivalent book. In scope and comprehensiveness it is broader than Marshall's *Principles*. In aims and objectives it is a challenge to all *dirigiste* thinkers, being a political platform as well as an analytic text. In it, according to his obituary, Mises highlighted his 'dissent from contemporary economists . . . who reacted by withholding many of the honours customarily bestowed on [the] master builders' of the profession.

If Mises evokes a feeling of tragedy at a personal level then Hayek does so (for Austrian economists) at the intellectual. Hayek left Austria, as did all of the 'Austrians' of the 1920s as a consequence of the fact or threat of National Socialism. He came to the London School of Economics in the 1930s and continued to develop his theories of the trade cycle (at a macro level) and prices as information (at a micro level) until the late 1940s. Sadly for Britain, and for economists as such, he turned his attention to philosophy when he left to work in the University of Chicago in the 1950s. Nonetheless, in the long term, his work on the *Constitution of Liberty* (1958) became a landmark, morally justifying many of his previous evoked economic views. These latter, however, were now ignored as a consequence of the apparent triumph of Keynesianism (at a macro-level) and 'indicative planning' (at a macro level). Not until the more naive forms of orthodox Keynesianism (as opposed to Keynes' own economic views) were challenged by the monetarists (such as Friedman) in the late 1960s and early 1970s did Hayek's earlier economic work again come to be regarded as worthy of note. The Nobel Prize followed in 1974.

Finally, we must note the modern day leader of Austrianism. If a name has to be singled out then, as an Austrian of the 1920s (*Ludwig Lachmann* who emigrated to Johannesburg to become the Professor of economics at the University of the Witwatersrand) pointed out in 1983 it must be that of *Israel Kirzner*. As a young member of the Mises New York seminars in the 1950s, and 1960s, it was he who unflinchingly held to and developed the Misesian viewpoint. It was he who had the most original and penetrating mind. And it is to Kirzner that most Austrians of the 1980's look as the man who 'Salvaged the Ideas' of Menger, Mises and Hayek. Ideas, which despite the stature of men such as *W H Hutt, Gottfried Haberler*, and (recent convert) *Sir John Hicks* or *G L S Shackle*, just might have been submerged by the alternative, even if not always unsympathetic, views of the post-Keynesian economics of the 1970s and 1980s.

Index